DEVELOPING REFERENCE COLLECTIONS AND SERVICES IN AN ELECTRONIC AGE

A How-To-Do-It Manual for Librarians

Kay Ann Cassell

HOW-TO-DO-IT MANUALS FOR LIBRARIANS

NUMBER 95

NEAL-SCHUMAN PUBLISHERS, INC.
New York, London

Published by Neal-Schuman Publishers, Inc.
100 Varick Street
New York, NY 10013

The paper used in this publication meets the minimum requirements of American National Standard for Information Sciences—Permanence of Paper for Printed Library Materials, ANSI Z39.48–1992. ∞

Printed and bound in the United States of America.

ISBN 1–55570–363–1

CONTENTS

List of Figures   vii

Preface   ix

Introduction   1
     Changing Reference Collections   3
     Adapting Budget Allocations   4
     Reference Service Patterns   5
     Changing Staff Needs   6
     Users and User Education   8
     The Future of Reference Service   8
     Notes   9

Chapter 1: The Changing Face of Reference Collections   11
     Reference Sources by Format   11
         Print Sources   12
         CD-ROM Sources   14
         Commercial Database Sources   16
         Internet Sources   18
     Reference Sources by Type of Material   25
         Encyclopedias   26
         Dictionaries, Thesauri, and Quotation Books   28
         Directories   29
         Atlases   30
         Biographical Source Locators   31
         Government Information Sources   32
         Indexes   33
     Reference Sources by Subject   35
         The Sciences   35
         The Social Sciences   37
         The Humanities   40
     Tools for Developing Reference Collections   43
         Internet Directories and Evaluative Guides   44
     Notes   46

Chapter 2: Changing Reference Service Patterns and Models   47

    In-Library Reference Service   48

        Academic Library Models   48

        Public Library Models   50

        Staffing Patterns   51

        Roving Reference Assistance   51

        Making Reference More User-Friendly   53

    Telephone Reference Service   54

    Electronic Reference Service   57

        Policy Considerations   58

        Form Design and Use   59

        E-mail Reference Service Models   60

    New Reference Service Challenges   64

        Distance Learning Programs   64

        Technical Support for Users   73

        The Future: Constant Change   73

    Notes   74

Chapter 3: User and Staff Education Needs   75

    Ways of Providing User Education   76

        Self-Help Guides and Tutorials   76

        Individual Instruction   78

        Group Instruction   79

        Distance Learning   83

        Models for Teaching Specific Skills   83

        The Future of User Education   89

    Planning for Staff Education   91

    Notes   93

Chapter 4: Planning for the Future   95

    Collection Evaluation and Deselection   96

    Collection Development Policy Considerations   98

        Formats   98

        Reliability of the Publisher   99

        Currency   99

        Relationship of Print and Electronic Sources   99

        Ease of Use   99

        Access Issues   99

        Technical Compatibility   100

Cost and Pricing 100

Use, Demand, and Redundancy 101

Cooperative Collection Development and

Consortial Arrangements 101

Access Development Policies 112

Reference Service Evaluation Methods 114

Surveys 114

Focus Groups 116

Other Methods 118

Putting All the Pieces Together in a Plan 118

Materials 118

Services 119

Personnel 119

Budget 120

Marketing 121

Final Thoughts 121

Notes 124

Bibliography 125

Reference Resources Cited 129

Index 133

About the Author 139

LIST OF FIGURES

1–1   Fort Worth Public Library: Criteria for selecting Internet
        resources   20

2–1   San Francisco Public Library e-mail reference service   61

2–2   Redwood City Public Library: Forms Online   63

2–3   Distance Learners Library Services   66

2–4   Sample electronic reference request form   70

2–5   Sample e-mail reference request form   72

3–1   Sample homepage leading to tutorial   77

3–2   Checklist for an advocacy Web page   85

3–3   Checklist for a business/marketing Web page   87

3–4   Beginner's Guide to the World Wide Web   90

4–1   Evaluating electronic resources   97

4–2   Sample electronic resources policy: The Tampa-
        Hillsborough County Public Library System   102

4–3   Sample electronic resources policy: Morton Grove
        Public Library   106

4–4   Sample electronic resources policy: Blue Ridge
        Regional Library   108

4–5   Sample electronic resources policy: Virginia Beach Public
        Library, Collection Management Manual   109

4–6   International Coalition of Library Consortia Statement   123

PREFACE

Libraries are changing. This is especially true in the reference department where both resources and services are undergoing massive changes. In many libraries, electronic reference materials and the electronic ways of delivering services (primarily e-mail and Web-based reference desks) are already irrevocably integrated with print-based collections and traditional services. This is an exciting time for reference librarians as old models are discarded and new ones developed. A special challenge for those of us involved in reference services is to plan for adapting our collections and services rather than to simply respond to technological changes.

I wrote *Developing Reference Collections and Services in an Electronic Age* to help librarians effectively plan to position their reference departments so they are poised to continuously adapt to new formats and meet new user expectations. The most successful planning involves two main components. The first is a holistic approach; all the components involved in delivering reference services must be considered—materials cannot be isolated from service delivery or from library instruction. The second is obtaining input from service users. Do core users think the library is moving too fast or too slowly in adding new electronic materials and services? What do users want when they come to the library? And what do they want when they access library information from remote locations?

Developing Reference Collections and Services in an Electronic Age is meant to provide librarians with a blueprint for developing a plan that meets their own users' expectations. The most successful plans will encompass balanced collection development, new or enhanced reference services, and improved library instruction—all based on input from the library's users. Effective plans will consider the crucial questions in the previous paragraph; each library's answers to these questions will vary depending on their resources users' expectations and needs. For example, some libraries will rely almost exclusively on electronic materials while others continue to maintain sizable print collections. To help address these differences, this manual includes numerous examples of collection development and reference service policies from a wide variety of libraries.

Developing Reference Collections and Services in an Electronic Age is divided into four chapters. Chapter 1 provides guidance to librarians deciding what format (print, CD-ROM, commercial database, or Web-based) to select for a specific title or category of material by enumerating and describing the strong and weak points of each format. This chapter also provides an overview of the range of materials available in digital formats by both type of material and by subject area.

Chapter 2 describes some of the changes in the way reference services are structured and illustrates them with examples of how specific libraries have experimented with new service patterns and implemented new procedures. The service patterns discussed include in-person reference services, telephone services, fax services, and electronic services (such as e-mail based reference).

Chapter 3 details very practical—and successful—approaches to user education in this new environment. The methods described range from working one-on-one to offering group instruction to providing user instruction for distance learners. Whether the users come into the library or use the library's Web site, they will always need instruction in using reference resources.

Chapter 4 provides a way of pulling these components together in order to develop a holistic plan for responding to change. Particular attention is paid to writing an electronic collection development policy and using surveys and focus groups to determine want and need. Examples of easily adaptable electronic collection development policies, surveys, and focus group questions are included to help readers implement the suggested process.

The process of writing a book today is different from in the past. The advent of listservs provides the writer with a way to gather information (especially examples) not available in books or articles. I want to thank the members of PubLib for providing me with useful information about what they were doing. I want to thank my partner, Marina Mercado, for her patience and support. I also want to thank Charles Harmon of Neal-Schuman Publishers for keeping me on track and giving me realistic deadlines.

Kay Ann Cassell
October 1999

INTRODUCTION

Library leaders want the library of the future to be a hybrid institution that contains both digital and book collections. And they assume that it will be the librarian "navigator" who will guide library users to the most useful sources, unlocking the knowledge and information contained in the vast annals of the information superhighway. Some library leaders envision a digital "library without walls" in which users gain access to almost unlimited amounts of information through home computers or at remote terminals located around the community. They also envision a time when one library's collection will, because of growing electronic capabilities, become everyone's collection.[1]

These opening phrases from a recent report prepared by the Benton Foundation set the stage for this book's discussion of how libraries are changing—especially reference collections and reference service—and how they are integrating the new electronic information resources into this service. This is an exciting time for reference librarians; it is an era of great change as old models are discarded and new ones developed. Reference service certainly will not disappear; library users continue to need advice and assistance in identifying the appropriate information resources, but some aspects of traditional reference service will end. How far the pendulum will swing from the present service is yet to be determined. It is certain, however, that access to information in so many formats and the increasing shift to electronic resources will significantly impact the development of reference service. In fact, "electronic resources have increased the use of reference services, increased time spent with individual users, increased need for staff training, increased staff time spent on troubleshooting, and increased need for user instruction."[2] The increased time spent with users is due to several factors, including user expectations that an answer can be found to any question, and the time required to help the user look for the answer in the vast array of materials—print and electronic—available.

As new technology provides access to material outside the library and allows for new and easier ways of searching, librarians must concentrate on their role as information managers and focus on how best to provide information to their users. Library collections and services obviously will be more fluid, and librarians will continue to provide value-added services that the users will need in order to use the many available information sources in an organized and efficient way. These services include customization and personalization of services delivered in whatever formats the user requires.

Many issues relate to the changes in reference service, and they must be carefully examined if the library is to serve its users well.

- Collections are changing. New reference materials need to be added to the library's collection, and many are available in more than one format. Librarians must decide on a case-by-case basis what format to choose for each reference source.
- Budget must be carefully considered. New and often expensive items may be beyond the limitations of the materials budget. It may be easier to add a new budget line for electronic information (such as databases available through the World Wide Web and CD-ROMs) than to increase the present materials budget. Librarians also can explore alternative ways of financing electronic resources, such as consortial arrangements to share costs.
- New patterns of reference service must be developed to incorporate the new electronic technologies in ways that make the best use of librarians' skills and expertise and that serve users more effectively. This may include front-line service by paraprofessionals and keeping librarians available for more in-depth assistance.
- Space must be found to house the new technology close to the reference area. In the future, reference departments will be designed differently, but for the present it may be that workstations must replace tables.
- Staff must be trained to deal with electronic resources that often require cooperation between the reference staff and other library staff dealing with technology or staff hired by the library's parent institution to deal with technology. Unless the staff is comfortable with the new technology, they cannot introduce it to their users. Continual staff training will be needed to keep them current.
- Users must be educated to handle the many new electronic resources. User education is more important in this new environment than ever before.

Some of the changes needed are easily accomplished, but others require more sophisticated hardware and software, more staff and user training. Some libraries have the infrastructure to easily implement new technology, whereas others have to find the funding to put the infrastructure in place. As some practices are abandoned and new ones are adapted, planning and staff training are necessary. Change is always difficult, and this decade of technological change has been so rapid that librarians have had a difficult time keeping pace. Computers must be constantly upgraded in order to run new, more sophisticated programs. The new electronic information resources produced last year may be replaced by other resources or, at the very least, new alternatives or upgrades will be available. Libraries must be prepared to deal with the number and accelerated rate of changes occurring in financial, technological, political, social/demographic, and cultural areas.

In the new information environment, the focus will change from ownership of information to access to information. More attention will be paid to evaluating what the users need and how libraries can meet their needs. The users are all important in this change. The University Licensing Program (TULIP), which lasted from 1991 to 1995 and involved Elsevier Science and nine American universities, studied how users would adapt to more access to electronic materials. Its goal was to test both the systems for networked delivery and for access of journals by users in these institutions. The material consisted of the ASCII full texts of 43 Elsevier and Pergamon science and engineering journals. Test results showed that users had the following requirements: "Ease to use, access to all information from one source, effective search capabilities, high processing speed, high publishing speed (timeliness), good image text quality, sufficient journal and time coverage and linking of information."[3] The study's results have implications well beyond this project and no doubt indicate what most if not all library users want and need. Of particular interest are the observations that providing large masses of digital information was expensive and that the infrastructure of the library was the key to whether it was possible to implement this provision. Also of interest is that "users will only move to electronic publications when they find the content they need in sufficient quantity . . . to warrant learning a new system and accessing information in a different way."[4]

CHANGING REFERENCE COLLECTIONS

The introduction of so many electronic reference sources in libraries has forced librarians to rethink reference collections. More options are available to librarians than ever before, and the number of new resources grows daily. It is both an exciting and challenging time. Librarians who already have had to stretch their budgets to buy necessary print materials now must also purchase electronic resources, adding new costs for items such as CD-ROMS, leased electronic databases, computers, and printers.

Many reference tools are now available in more than one format—

print, microform, CD-ROM, online, or on the Internet. Librarians must choose the format(s) appropriate for their situation. The decision depends on the users' needs, the formats they prefer, and what formats the library can support. But many other factors enter into these decisions. They include the appropriateness of the content for the format chosen, the demand for the information, the cost (which may include software and equipment), the space available for any additional equipment, the time needed to install the new electronic reference tool, its learning curve—for both librarians and users—and the format(s) preferred by the users. Chapter 1 will discuss these formats, their characteristics, and evaluation criteria.

Although it may seem that libraries could settle on one format, this is not necessarily so. The new formats often do not include much retrospective material. Full-text indexes are a prime example of this. The producer of the CD-ROM, online, or World Wide Web version often chooses to include only a few retrospective years. Even though the text of a journal is available through a subscription to the full-text index, the library must continue to buy the journal in paper or microform if it wants to have a complete run of a journal. Since there is no guarantee that any vendor of a full-text index will be able to continue to supply the full text, many libraries' costs have increased due to providing information in the electronic format as well as another format so as to have a lasting record.

Not all materials subscribed to by the library will be housed in the library. Indexes and other reference materials are often available on the World Wide Web. Other materials are available through online services. Libraries must decide how to handle this material since it needs to be listed or cataloged so that users will know it is available.

A collection-development policy for electronic resources is essential both to help the librarians develop consistent practices and to have a document for use with governmental or institutional officials and the library's users. The elements of this policy will be discussed in depth in chapter 4.

ADAPTING BUDGET ALLOCATIONS

Library budgets are not funded for the addition of so many electronic resources. Most libraries, already budgeting carefully just to manage their small library materials budgets, are feeling the financial strain of new electronic resources and have been forced to rethink their budgets. Libraries may have to choose between print and electronic resources, even though issues such as archiving of electronic resources are not clear. They may have to have less variety in the materials purchased in order to afford the same titles in more than one format.

One route has been to develop a separate budget line for electronic resources and to convince the governing body or funding agency to establish this new line and increase the library's budget. Once a new budget line is established, it becomes easier to gradually increase it while retaining the budget line for print materials. Another route is to enter into consortial arrangements with other libraries. Sharing the cost of electronic databases can help tremendously in cost-saving. Some libraries are forming consortia just for this purpose, whereas others are using existing cooperative arrangements and adding database purchases to their activities. Some states have even taken on the task of negotiating prices for statewide access to certain databases. OhioLink, funded by the state of Ohio, provides a wide variety of electronic databases to Ohio libraries (see chapter 4 for more information on it).

REFERENCE SERVICE PATTERNS

Many factors besides electronic reference tools have brought about the extraordinary changes in reference service, such as changes in the way users look for and handle information. Users want more current information, and increasing numbers of them want to find it all on a computer screen so that they can print it out and take it with them. Electronic tools have given users the impression that they don't need a library or librarian since they can find full-text material on the Internet, can do research from home or the office without even going to the library, and can access electronic tools from remote locations. By default, these are becoming preferred sources and often the only sources a user consults. This means that libraries have to develop some method of communication to support remote users and computer-based instruction on their Web site to assist those users in using the library's resources.

Ironically, however, users also expect more of library staff in this electronic environment. They expect librarians to know about all the electronic resources the library has and to help the users learn to use them quickly. They also expect faster service because the electronic atmosphere gives the impression of speed and infinite possibility. According to Richard Sweeney, library director at the New Jersey Institute of Technology, "Library users desire a wide range of alternative, customized service options, self-service, and universal accessibility and availability. Users want convenient, easy continuous service access, 24 hours per day, 365 days per year, from anywhere. Users want the power to decide when, where, and how to obtain access to a library service. They even want to determine the level of library service they should receive."[5]

However, estimates are that a very small percent of the information in print has been digitized—probably no more than 10 percent. Librarians must communicate this reality to their public. They must expand their users' views of library resources and encourage them to use many different materials in many formats.

Library services will indeed expand with the advent of so much new technology. Libraries will be asked to deliver services by fax, e-mail, the Internet, and telephone to more users who cannot or choose not to come to the physical library. New techniques must be developed to interview and assist those users in finding the materials they need. Libraries must also decide how to transmit information to users who are not near the physical library. Options include regular mail, e-mail, overnight mail services, and fax.

New services will develop as collections are shared electronically and accessed remotely. Libraries will set up new cooperative arrangements with other libraries to continue to serve users well. They must decide how to share materials and whether they will charge fees or develop a mutually acceptable agreement.

New physical layouts of reference service areas must be developed. Libraries need more space for computer workstations as well as space where users can consult and use print materials. New models of reference service discussed in chapter 2 may also influence the design of this area.

Marketing will be another important aspect in the development of new services. Electronic resources and services are not as immediately visible as traditional library services, so librarians will have to develop new ways to advertise them to their users.

CHANGING STAFF NEEDS

As reference service changes, so does the role of the reference librarian. First, the reference librarian is required to have more knowledge than ever before. The librarian must be familiar with an increasing number of reference sources in print, on CD-ROM, online, and on the Internet. Second, the librarian must be able to select and evaluate reference sources in all formats and to determine both the quality of the sources and their feasibility in a particular library setting. Third, the librarian must identify and organize the resources available on the Internet that are appropriate for the library's users. New tools must be designed that will provide the library's users with easy access to resources. Fourth, the librarian must be knowledgeable about technology and know enough about equipment to troubleshoot basic problems. Fifth, the librarian must become expert in user education—instructing library users and developing library-use instruction. Finally, the librarian must be able to market and publicize the resources and services of the library to maintain the library's visibility and thus encourage its use.

Staffing must also change as the result of technology. The original goal of technology to reduce staff size has not been realized. Instead, technology has brought about a redeployment of staff and the addition of staff with technological expertise. The clear-cut delineation between professional and nonprofessional staff has blurred as technical staff has been hired with the same level of education as librarians. For example, libraries are hiring staff with bachelor's and master's degrees in computer studies to assist with the technical end of computers and others with degrees in educational technology to provide a new point of view and to develop online tutorials. Libraries also have begun to employ another kind of staff in a paraprofessional or page category who can be trained to help users with the basics of OPACs (online public access catalogs), electronic resources, and the Internet. Many patrons are not accustomed to using computers and need assistance in getting started. Librarians, though willing to assist, have found themselves overwhelmed and are not able both to continue quality reference service and to provide technical assistance.

The new technology has made staff development an increasingly important issue. Training has become an integral part of library work, and staff skills must be continually upgraded. Librarians and other staff must learn how to use new equipment and become familiar with new databases. As hard as libraries try to stay ahead with training, it has become all too common that new databases are added to the OPACs and the librarians are put in the position of learning the database along with the users. As this issue is addressed, more funds will be spent on staff training in order to keep them up-to-date with new databases and changes in search strategies.

USERS AND USER EDUCATION

Libraries will become more client centered in this new technological environment. They will use a variety of evaluation methods—focus groups, written surveys, interviews, and informal means, for example—to determine better what their users want. Librarians also will need to learn more about how their varied users want to receive and then use information so that they can shape services to meet needs.

Users themselves are demanding more. Electronic resources seem somehow easier to use. Libraries find that when electronic tools are introduced, it is hard to get users to go back to print sources even when they are more appropriate—or even only available—in print. The users' love affair with electronic services is so all encompassing that some users think all research can be done sitting at a terminal. In reality, users need a great deal of education and assistance to be able to use the new electronic tools effectively and efficiently. Studies have shown that most users do not try the more sophisticated search strategies and, in fact, barely understand basic search strategies. There is much more to learn to get the most out of the electronic products. Librarians often spend more time orienting users than when only print resources were available. This may be in a small group setting or one-to-one. The librarian may play a collaborative role working with the user to design a search on an online service and evaluate the results. Chapter 3 discusses user training in more detail.

THE FUTURE OF REFERENCE SERVICE

Librarians must be continually developing and implementing new services more quickly than ever before. They can do this successfully if they are continually alert to possibilities and opportunities.

"Many prognosticators of the electronic future contend that the library as a place is as ephemeral as electronic technology itself. There will be no need for a building, and to think there is misses what the electronic future is all about. Instead, there will be a constantly evolving network of elements. If you are a technobeliever, the 'network' will be the library of the future."[6] There are, in fact, plans to build colleges and universities without libraries in the traditional sense. But this approach is probably not a realistic option for most libraries for many years to come. In fact, many think that the future includes library buildings because humans need to work and learn in a supportive environment. Whatever the future holds, for the present libraries will continue to be a mix of the traditional and the new. Digital information will be integrated into paper-based library collections. Library users will continue to need guidance in using library materials in all formats and in choosing materials appropriate to their needs and interests. Most change will be gradual; some subject areas will have many more reference tools in digital formats sooner than others. Obviously, print collections will shrink as more material becomes available in digital format. But for many reasons, users will prefer a mixture of formats. Many reference tools are faster to use in print format. For example, checking the address, phone number, and the name of the executive director of a nonprofit organization or ascertaining the capital of an African country will probably be fastest in a print directory. The print reference source may be easier to use for certain other questions, but for more sophisticated searching the indexing available on a CD-ROM or an online source may be helpful. For example, to find the author of a book, the print version of *Books in Print* is sufficient. But if you know only part of the book's title, which turns out to be a subtitle, you will only find it by searching *Books in Print* electronically. Each reference tool must be evaluated since the transfer from one format to another often brings changes—some positive, some negative. For example, a newspaper or magazine on CD-ROM may be easier to use, but all the articles may not be indexed, making it less than adequate for many users.

Libraries must face many issues, including the fact that not all resources will be in the library building. Remote resources and collections will be an integral part of the resources offered to the users, and thus reference service will not be so self-contained. The priority will be on access and service rather than on site collections. Our focus will be getting the information to the user, wherever the user is. Yet libraries will still be needed for their many value-added services and users will continue to need the individualized assistance the librarian can provide.

NOTES

1. Benton Foundation, *Buildings, Books, and Bytes* (Washington, D.C.: Benton Foundation, 1996), 4.
2. Carol Tenopir, "Reference Use Statistics," *Library Journal* (May 1, 1998): 32.
3. TULIP Final Report, executive summary [online] available at: *www.elsevier.nl/homepage/about/resproj/trmenu.htm*

4. TULIP Final Report.
5. Richard Sweeney, "Leadership Skills in the Reengineered Library: Empowerment and Value Added Trend? Implications for Library Leaders," *Library Administration and Management* 11 (winter 1997): 31–32.
6. Larry Dowler, "Our Edifice at the Precipice," *Library Journal* (February 15, 1996): 118.

1 THE CHANGING FACE OF REFERENCE COLLECTIONS

Library collections, especially reference collections, are changing rapidly as more and more electronic resources become available. Although most people prefer to read a novel or work of nonfiction in print format, electronic formats are ideal for reference materials in which people are reading shorter amounts of information or just looking up a fact or statistic. Because many reference materials are available in electronic formats, librarians must continually read reviews and test new products to determine their appropriateness for the reference collection. Today's best sources may be out-of-date tomorrow, as software publishers produce new and better products. Librarians must continue to buy new materials and update their collections based on the most accurate current information as well as on an examination of new materials whenever possible. Waiting for the perfect product is just not realistic.

The proliferation of electronic resources does not mean that print resources will vanish. In fact, some resources always will be best in print format; others will be developed in electronic format and will never be published in print. The challenge for librarians is twofold: to compare similar materials in different formats and decide which formats are best for the library, and to select the best materials available. Many reference resources are bundled together in an electronic format, so the librarian must examine carefully what is being offered. This bundling of resources presents difficulties for librarians who are accustomed to making decisions on a title-by-title basis. Decisions about format and content cannot be the same for all libraries. Many factors enter into the decision including issues of space, available technology and infrastructure, cost, and user preferences and needs.

REFERENCE SOURCES BY FORMAT

Each format—print, CD-ROM, online, and the Internet—lends itself to certain kinds of uses. To generalize that all materials will or should be in one format does not consider variations in use. Sometimes the information itself is better suited to one format, and sometimes the needs of the library and its users dictate the format. In this chapter, each format will be examined as to its features, its advantages and disadvantages, the criteria for selection, and the availability of quality products in the format. The reader should note that "one size does not fit all—what is selected for one library may not be appropriate for another.

PRINT SOURCES

Print sources have been the standard format for most reference materials and still are used widely by reference librarians. Their advantage is that no additional equipment is needed to use them. Librarians can simply buy the book or other printed matter, catalog it, process it, and shelve it. Print is readily available to consult when not in use by others. Multivolume works can be shared by several users at the same time. For many reference sources, print is the best and only available format. It is straightforward, uncomplicated, and requires no technological skills. The user can consult the table of contents or index and go quickly to the appropriate section, or can browse through the book to find the needed information.

A reference book's usefulness depends on its content, its arrangement, how well it is indexed, and how up-to-date it is. Some books contain a great deal of useful information, but their internal organization makes them difficult to use. For example, a book may use a topical arrangement that is hard to understand or have indexes that are incomplete and detract from the usefulness of the work. Because many reference books are expensive to revise and update, much of the information they contain may be erroneous or obsolete by the time new editions are published. Printed materials also are vulnerable to theft and damage.

Print resources published in volumes can be awkward and time consuming to use if the reader has to consult successive volumes. Periodical indexes are a good example of this. Print indexes must be consulted volume-by-volume, because cumulative volumes are published only at intervals. If many years must be consulted, the user can take a considerable period of time to do the required research.

Print reference resources should be evaluated according to the following criteria:

- content and coverage of the subject
- accuracy of the information
- objectivity of the information
- authority/reputation of the author and publisher
- currency of the information
- organization of the information
- price
- quality of binding
- page layout (including typeface)

The treatment of the material in the reference book is important. The librarian must determine if the subject has been adequately covered or whether some important aspects have been omitted. Analyzing the coverage of the subject also leads to an analysis of the objectivity of the information provided, as well its accuracy and currency; many fine-looking reference works are filled with errors. Because of the need for accuracy in reference materials, it is important to ascertain the author's expertise in the subject area of the book. The publisher's credentials are equally important. Many publishers specialize in certain areas of reference publishing and have a good track record for producing books of quality by expert authors. For example, a publisher might specialize in biographical directories (Marquis, for example), atlases (Rand McNally, for example), or indexes (H. W. Wilson, for example). The organization of the material is important to the usefulness of the reference book. A good table of contents and index, as well as a clear, easy to understand arrangement of the contents, will help the user locate specific pieces of information. Finally, the book should be fairly priced and in line with the pricing of similar reference works. The quality of the binding is important because libraries prefer to buy books that last a reasonable amount of time. The pages should be designed so that there is enough white space to make them comfortable for the reader. A clear, easy to read typeface is also essential—a small typeface often discourages the user.

Although it would seem that printed reference books might disappear with the advent of CD-ROMs and the Internet, they still sell well even when an electronic version is available. "For now, publishers are still confident that printed reference can't be beat; that computer research may be handy but that nothing can top the convenience of an open volume, pages bursting with information ready at hand to inform, entertain and brighten the pathway to learning."[1] However, many continue to forecast the end of books as we know them. In fact, one analyst has stated that "half of what's now in book form (that is, sheets of paper somehow bound into volumes) could be replaced by digital publishing and distribution. . . . [b]y replacing most or all of the parts catalogs, operating manuals, maintenance guides and similar items that aren't meant to be read end to end."[2] This has not happened and probably will not happen in the foreseeable future due to the popularity of print and the cost and availability of adequate equipment for CD-ROMs and the Internet. In fact, publishers have found that having a reference book available on the Web actually encourages sales of the print version.

CD-ROM SOURCES

CD-ROMs are a popular electronic format for two reasons. First, they can store a large amount of information in a small amount of space; second, they offer Boolean searching, thus assisting the user in finding additional material that might not be so easily located in a print format. They are especially suited for multivolume reference works whose many volumes can be integrated on one disc, and for directories where many different pieces of information within an entry can be searched separately or at once. For example, the *1998 Writer's Market* on CD-ROM can be searched by many categories at one time, thus enabling a writer to look for potential publications in a targeted manner. Searches can be developed to find publication sources by type of material (for example, fiction, nonfiction), circulation, subject, pay rate, rights' issues, and so forth. CD-ROMs are a good choice for reference sources with a limited audience. They take up less space and yet provide the needed access. For example, the CD-ROM version of the fifth edition of *Famous First Facts* allows searching by keyword, subject, name, city, state, and date, thereby allowing the user quickly to find the needed information. Many CD-ROMs are interactive and enable the user to move from one aspect of a subject to another. CD-ROMs also have the capacity to provide video and sound, which enhance the presentation. For example, the *Encarta Encyclopedia Deluxe Edition* has both video and sound clips. *The American Sign Language Dictionary* has video clips demonstrating each sign, which greatly enhances the usefulness of the dictionary.

The CD-ROM may be easier for some users than the Internet because a CD-ROM's retrieval rate is not affected by the slowness that libraries experience on the Internet during heavily used time periods. However, the librarian must decide if a CD-ROM provides useful additional features or if it is just the same book in a new format. For example, a review of the *Computer Desktop Encyclopedia* stated: "Why bother to put this on CD-ROM, when the arrangement is basically in book form: you scroll through a linear list of terms or jump to text in a linear page of text via a text search? A well-indexed book may make better sense, since it can be consulted without switching applications or multitasking."[3] There is little advantage in owning a CD-ROM with no value-added material. A recent review of the CD-ROM of *Emily Post's Complete Guide to Weddings* stated: "It takes two or three times as long to access the information here as it would in print, and, given the static nature of the content, there is no good reason for using the CD-ROM."[4] Therefore, libraries with limited equipment and space for equipment might choose not to add a CD-ROM when a book is sufficient. CD-ROMs are usually limited to one PC or to a local area network (LAN) and cannot accommodate many simultaneous users. This may be a deciding factor for libraries that need a large number of workstations.

Multidisc sets of CD-ROMs can be cumbersome and confusing for library users if they must switch back-and-forth between discs. Investigate also how current a CD-ROM is; even though it seems easier to update a CD-ROM, the producer sometimes puts the print reference source on CD-ROM with no updating and no plans to update it any more frequently than the print version of the book. Accuracy also must be considered. If the CD-ROM product was previously in book form, the librarian may be familiar with its accuracy, but if the reference book was developed as a CD-ROM product with no print edition, its accuracy and reliability must be evaluated carefully. Cost is another factor. If the CD-ROM has no value-added component, it may not be worth buying if it is more expensive than the book. Some CD-ROM products are easier to use than others, so it is important to determine if the user will find the protocols easy to learn to use or if the CD-ROM will just slow down the user's search for information. If the learning curve for a CD-ROM is too steep, neither the librarian nor the user will want to use it.

In conclusion, a CD-ROM must be evaluated as to:

- accuracy and reliability of the information
- objectivity of the information
- ease of searching, including clear and easy-to-use screens
- authority of the creator/author and the publisher
- currency of the information and the ability of the publisher to make timely updates to the information
- cost, especially as compared to the reference work in print
- presentation of the information and the accompanying graphics
- value-added features that distinguish it from the print product
- customer support, including operating manuals for the library staff and user guides for the public
- licensing agreement and restrictions

Major CD-ROM publishers and providers are:

- Bell & Howell Information and Learning (formerly UMI) (*www.umi.com*). Full-text CD-ROM databases include *ProQuest Direct, ABI/INFORM,* and *Dissertation Abstracts.*
- Chadwyck-Healey, Inc. (*www.chadwyck.com*). Databases include reference sources on history, literature, art, and political and social sciences such as *Literature Online, Digital National Security Archive, International Index to Music Periodicals Full Text,* and *International Index to the Performing Arts Full Text.*

- Congressional Quarterly, Inc. (*www.cq.com*). Titles include *CQ Researcher*, *Staff Directories on CD-ROM*, *Member Data Disk*, and *State Legislator Data Disk*.
- Dialog Corporation (*www.dialog.com*). Eighty databases available, including ones for business, humanities, education, and law.
- EBSCO Publishing (*www.epnet.com*). Full-text CD-ROM indexes for all types of libraries, including *Health Source*, *Business Source*, *Academic Abstracts FullTEXT Elite*, *Newspaper Source*, and *MAS FullTEXT* (MasterFILE Full TEXT).
- OVID Technologies, Inc. (*www.ovid.com*). Titles include *MEDLINE* and *CINAHL* (Cumulative Index to Nursing and Allied Health)
- R. R. Bowker (*www.bowker.com*). Titles include the *Books in Print* series, *Ulrich's on Disc*, *American Library Directory on Disc*, and *Literary Market Place on Disc*.
- SilverPlatter (*www.silverplatter.com/usa*). Databases cover business, science and technology, humanities, and social sciences. Many titles from other publishers are distributed through SilverPlatter.
- SIRS Mandarin, Inc. (*www.sirs.com*). Titles include *Researcher*, *Renaissance*, *Government Reporter*.
- H. W. Wilson (*www.hwwilson.com*). Publisher provides its indexes on CD-ROM with some full-text articles, includes the *Reader's Guide to Periodical Literature*, the *Humanities Index*, and the *Social Science Index*.

Many have predicted the demise of CD-ROMs, but these predictions have not come to pass so far. CD-ROMs continue to be a viable format. They are popular in small libraries that do not have the technology infrastructure to handle extensive online or Internet service. They are also especially popular in school libraries. *Library Journal* reported that " . . . the number of (new reference) CD-ROMs made a comeback to nearly 100 after last year's low of 70."[5]

A new development in reference publishing is the improved audio and video DVD (digital video disk)-ROM, whose increased disc capacity eliminates the need for multidisc sets. A number of reference titles are now available in DVD-ROM, including encyclopedias (*Britannica*, *Compton's*, and *World Book*) as well as *Phonefinder USA*, Delorme's *AAA Map 'n' Go*, and SilverPlatter's *MEDLINE Advanced*.

COMMERCIAL DATABASE SOURCES

Online commercial databases comprise another reference format. They include such commercial networks as Dialog, locally mounted databases, and access to databases from remote locations. Some CD-ROMs such as encyclopedias also have online components that update and enhance the information available on the CD-ROM.

Online is a useful format because:

1. It can handle large bibliographic and full-text databases.
2. It is easily updated. Any database that is updated frequently is better in an online format since it avoids the necessity of replacing the CD-ROM. For example, indexes and bibliographic databases work well online because of their size; reference sources such as directories work well online because of the need to update them frequently.
3. It allows the user to search several databases at one time, as is possible on Dialog and OCLC's *First Search*.
4. It can accommodate more simultaneous users than can a CD-ROM LAN.
5. It can provide access to a wider variety of databases, exceeding what can be offered on a CD-ROM LAN.
6. It can make the databases available to off-site users.

The new subscription packages for online services do make the need for increased use more economical. For example, many databases with full-text articles now offer users the option to tape-load the articles locally. This approach can be economical for a large library system, but the storage capacity of available computers must be evaluated to see if they can deal with growing databases.

Online resources should be evaluated using the following criteria:

- coverage of the subject
- accuracy of the information
- objectivity of the information
- authority of author/publisher
- currency of the information
- price
- ease of use/searching

Online databases frequently used in libraries include:

- Dialog, an online service with databases on practically every subject
- Dow Jones, a business database with business news from newspapers and magazines
- LEXIS-NEXIS, an online service that provides legal, general, and business information from magazines, newspapers, research reports, and newsletters

In the next few years, most online services will migrate to the Web. They will, of course, continue to charge fees for their databases, but the Web will provide them with the flexibility to use more multimedia, hypertext, and other enhancements.

INTERNET SOURCES

The Internet has become an important way to transmit information to users for a number of reasons.

1. It is a source of the most current information and can be updated quickly.
2. It is easy to use and does not require any additional equipment beyond the PC and modem.
3. It has the advantage of hypertext capability (the ability to link to other Web sites and bring together related information in one location).
4. It can add graphics, photographs, sound, video, and animation to a Web site.

The disadvantages of Internet sites are that they are not always accurate and up-to-date, they make users think that everything is available via the Web, and they can be slow to access when the Web is busy.

Internet sources consist of two types: free sources that have been developed by institutions, organizations, or individuals and are available to anyone searching the Web; and leased databases that are available through the Web for a fee.

Free Internet Sources

Since libraries' Web sites link to many free Internet sites, libraries must carefully evaluate them in the same way as any reference work and frequently reevaluate them to be sure their information is still up-to-date and reliable. The content of the site should be either unique, providing information not available elsewhere, or comprehensive. In other words, it should contribute in a significant way to a particular subject. Be sure you understand the scope of a site and its limits before linking to it; some sites have purposes other than providing information— perhaps marketing a particular product or point of view—and may not be appropriate for a library's Web site link. The sites chosen should be written in clear, nontechnical language that is free of grammatical and spelling errors. Graphics, sound, and video should enhance the site but not be so elaborate as to slow down the response time. The information should be accurate, and any biases or opinions clearly identified. The authorship must be checked to determine who produced the site and what the author's credentials are. This can provide some indication of the reliability of the site. There should also be an e-mail address to contact the author(s) of the site. The user should be able to tell when the site was last updated. Determining if the content is being updated and if links are valid requires frequent visits to the site. Sites should be designed for easy navigation; information should be easy to find, and there should be a consistent pattern from page to page. Many sites are well designed, but have little content to offer. Sometimes the design itself makes the site difficult to use because there is too much information or too much design producing clutter. Sites should be evaluated for the clarity of their instructions; can the user easily comprehend the scope of the site and how to use it?

A good way to evaluate the organization of the site is to see how many clicks it takes to get to the needed information. If more than three clicks are needed, then valuable information is buried too deep in the site, and the site needs more work. Search engines should be available to assist the user with both Boolean and keyword searching. Indexes make a site more useful, so determine if there is a searchable index. In summary, free Internet sites should be evaluated for the following:

- accuracy of the information
- objectivity of the information (clear attempt to state biases or opinions)
- authority of the Web site publisher (person responsible for the site)
- currency of the information (regular updating and few, if any, dead links)
- design and organization of the site
- cost (if any)
- contribution to the subject—uniqueness or comprehensiveness (scope should be clearly stated)
- length of time it takes to download a site
- navigation and ease of use
- ability to reach site (i.e., is it so busy it is hard to reach?)
- usefulness of search engines or indexes
- reliability and stability of the site (URL does not change)

Many libraries have developed criteria for selecting Internet sites for their own Web site. The Fort Worth (TX) Public Library has developed such criteria and included them in their collection development policy (see Figure 1–1 for those criteria).

Figure 1–1

FORT WORTH PUBLIC LIBRARY:
CRITERIA FOR SELECTING INTERNET RESOURCES

In accordance with the Forth Worth Public Library's Materials Collection Development Policy (Sec. VIA), the Internet Resources on the Library's homepage cover a wide variety of interests within many subject areas and attempt to provide a balanced representation of all ethnic/cultural backgrounds in all points of view on current and historical issues. The general collection level is to support advanced undergraduate or sustained independent study.

The following criteria will be used to select Internet resources:

CURRENCY

Site is updated periodically (depending on the nature of the information, that may need to be daily, weekly, monthly, but must be at least quarterly)

Site has date of last revision posted (reflects commitment to ongoing maintenance)

CONTENT/INFORMATION

Content fits within the scope of the FWPL Collection Development Policy

Vocabulary and reading level are appropriate for FWPL patrons

Depth/breadth of information is appropriate for FWPL patrons

Information is accurate when checked against other sources

Information is factual rather than opinion, and source is clearly stated

Text is easy-to-understand and has correct spelling/grammar

Any political or ideological biases toward subject matter are balanced by sites with other political or ideological views

Any graphics/sounds/videos serve a clear purpose & enhance site

AUTHORITY

The authors are clearly identifiable

The authors are authorities in their field (credentials offered)

The location or sponsor of site is identifiable

A mail-to-link or e-mail address is offered to contact authors

Caution will be used in linking to URLs with ~ because that indicates an individual's directory rather than an institution

EASE OF NAVIGATION

Site is arranged in a logical manner to facilitate locating information

Pages are attractive and encourage exploration

It is easy to navigate between pages

Layout is consistent from page to page

Users will find the site worth the time

ACCESSIBILITY
> Site connects quickly
> Site doesn't require special software or password to view
> URL is stable (doesn't change frequently)
> Graphics load quickly
> Text-only, graphical and non-frames versions offered to user

MISCELLANEOUS
> Site has won a recognized Internet award (Top 5%, Best of the Web, etc.), been reviewed positively in a professional/trade journal or been recommended by subject expert
> Site may not charge connection fee but may charge the user a fee to access their information database
> Site may not be for profit (is the site's primary purpose to sell something?)
> Internet Resources pages are checked monthly for connectivity and evaluated at least quarterly using the above criteria.

Reprinted with the permission of the Fort Worth Public Library.

Even though the Internet would appear to be the best way to access ready reference information, it is not always so. Recent studies indicate that some questions can be quickly and accurately answered via the Internet, but others are much faster to answer using a book. It will take the experience and good judgment of librarians to decide where to go first. In the immediate future, many librarians will agree with Chuck Koutnik who concluded that for the time being librarians will continue to rely on printed reference books to answer many reference questions.[6] The Internet is a useful reference source, but it must be used in combination with print sources.

Combining print and Web information is an important skill. For example, if the user need a great deal of information on a subject, it may be necessary to use print sources that provide more in-depth coverage than can be found on the Web. The best reference work on the subject may not be available on the Web. At other times, the information on the Web may be current but may not have the retrospective information the user needs and print sources may be needed to supplement the Web sites. For example, a great deal of biographical information is in print sources, but in order to completely answer a question about a living person, the Internet should be consulted to bring the print source up-to-date. A great deal of historical information is only available in print format, yet very recent writings (such as speeches and news reports) may be most easily found on the Internet.

To assist library users who are interested in using Web sites on the

Internet, many libraries have developed homepages that point to sites the library has selected. By selecting and monitoring sites, the library can do with the Web what it has done with the rest of its collection: it selects and makes available to its users its recommended information sites. Usually the library organizes the recommended sites by subject so the user can easily browse the homepage and identify interesting sites—such as business information, government resources, cultural institutions, current events and news, job and career resources, health information. Good examples of library homepages are the Redwood City (CA) Public Library (*www.ci.redwood-city.ca.us/library/rcpl.html*) and the Seattle (WA) Public Library (*www.spl.lib.wa.us*). The Redwood City homepage includes a useful "Frequently Asked Reference Questions" page linking the user to Internet information including car prices, baby names, genealogy and postal information, and a page of forms enabling the user to ask reference questions and request interlibrary loans. The Seattle homepage includes a ready reference section for zip codes, area codes, awards, calendars, directories, statistics, time, weather, and more, and a Web site index by subject as well as a monthly newsletter, *Read On: What's News at the Seattle Public Library*. The newsletter includes a calendar of events for the month and highlights new and ongoing services. Gerry McKiernan, science and technology librarian and bibliographer, Iowa State University Library, maintains a Web site, "Beyond Bookmarks: Schemes for Organizing the Web" (*www.public.istate.edu/~CYBERSTACKS/CTW.htm*) described on the site as a "clearinghouse of World Wide Web sites that have applied or adopted standard classification schemes or controlled vocabularies to organize or provide enhanced access to Internet resources." A useful guide to classification schemes already in use, it includes the Dewey Decimal Classification, the Library of Congress Subject Headings, the Universal Decimal Classification, and the National Library of Medicine subject headings.

John Lubans Jr., deputy university librarian at the Duke University's Lilly Library, conducted a study to find out how first-year students were using the library. The results showed that 85 percent were using the Web for educational purposes. Based on this, Lubans suggests that librarians should take a more active role in identifying and recommending useful and informational Web sites. He is a strong advocate of adding relevant Web sites, with hot links, to the library's online catalog.[7] Indeed, academic libraries have gone even further than public libraries in searching out Web sites and developing Web pages on a subject-by-subject basis (anthropology, biology, literature, history, and so on) to help their users find relevant material on topics of interest. Good examples of university library Web sites are those of the University of California at Berkeley Library (*www.lib.berkeley.edu/*), which provides an extensive list of subjects and Internet sites to search and the University at Albany Libraries (*www.albany.edu/library/*), which lists Internet subject directories and also includes a list by subject of both Internet resources and electronic databases.

A number of national projects are working to identify recommended sites and to organize them by subject, for example, OCLC's NetFirst. NetFirst is a subject approach to Internet-accessible resources using the hierarchical structure of the Dewey Decimal Classification, but not its class numbers, to classify Web sites. California has the Librarians' Index to the Internet (LII), a subject directory to over 4,000 Internet sites, developed first under the auspices of the Berkeley Public Library and now the UC-Berkeley Digital Library SunSITE (*sunsite.berkeley.edu/InternetIndex/*). The oldest of the projects to organize the Internet is the Internet Public Library (IPL) at the University of Michigan's School of Information (*www.ipl.org*), an extensive site also organized by subject. Best Information on the Net (BIOTIN), at the O'Keefe Library at St. Ambrose University (*www.sau.edu/CWIS/Internet/Wild/index.htm*), provides links to useful information for librarians. INFOMINE is an academic library site originally started at the University of California, Riverside, that is organized by LC subject headings (*informine.ucr.edu/Main.html*).[8] Individual librarians also have put up useful Web sites pointing to Internet sites they recommend. For example, Anne Prestamo's homepage, Web Resources for Libraries (*www.library.okstate.edu/dept/sed/prestamo/anne1.HTM)*, is arranged by several large subject areas: business and finance, law and government, education resources, Latin American/Spanish language resources, classical music resources, reference sources, and services to librarians. Each section points to many useful resources. Many new projects continue to emerge as librarians focus on the need to manage effectively the resources on the Internet.

Leased Electronic Databases on the Internet

The second type of Internet resources available through the World Wide Web are databases leased by the library or by a consortium. A number of publishers of reference sources have put their materials on the Web, which can be particularly useful resources if the library's users want to access the information from remote sites. The downside of accessing databases this way is that the sites may be slow and hard to reach during the parts of the day when traffic on the Internet is heaviest. The library must determine if the publisher's contract allows for multiple access points, whether remote access is possible, and whether there are any other contract stipulations preventing the library from having sufficient access to the database. Of course, the library must also decide if the subscription is worth the fee and if the library can provide enough access (enough workstations and access for remote users) to make the fee worth paying.

Criteria for selection of leased databases should include:

- accuracy and reliability of the content, especially if the reference source originated in an electronic format
- currency of information
- ease of searching
- reasonable access time during peak Internet hours
- value-added features such as the ability to customize the database
- customer support
- a workable licensing agreement
- cost in relation to the same source in other formats

Reference publishers with products available through the World Wide Web and providers of Web-based reference materials include:

- Bell & Howell Information and Learning (formerly UMI) (*www.umi.com*). Publisher of indexes with full-text articles on the Web including *Proquest*.
- R. R. Bowker (*www.bowker.com*). Publisher of *Books in Print, Ulrich's International Periodicals Directory*, the *American Library Directory*, and other reference materials.
- Chadwyck-Healey, Inc. (*www.chadwyck.com*). Publisher of literature, history, art, social and political science databases such as *Literature Online*.
- Congressional Quarterly, Inc. (*www.cq.com*). Publisher of information on government, politics, and public policy.
- Dialog Corporation (*www.dialog.com*). Provider of DialogClassic, a Web interface to its traditional online service.
- Dun and Bradstreet Information Services (*www.dnb.com*). Publisher of the *Million Dollar Directory*.
- EBSCO Publishing (*www.epnet.com*). Publisher of full-text indexes for all types of libraries including *Health Source* and *Business Source*.
- Facts on File (*www.factsonfile.com*). Publisher of reference materials on contemporary issues, science, history, health and medicine, religion and mythology, and many other subjects, many of which are on the Web, including *World News Digest*.
- Gale Group (*www.gale.com*). Publisher of a wide array of standard reference tools, many of which are on the Web including the *Encyclopedia of Associations, Contemporary Authors*, and *Ready Reference Shelf*.

- Moody's Financial Information Services, available on the Web as Moody's Company DataDirect (*www.moodys.com*).
- Lexis-Nexis (*www.lexis-nexis.com*). Provides legal information, news articles, current events, and business information.
- SIRS Mandarin, Inc. (*www.sirs.com*). Publisher of educational resources, whose reference materials include selected full-text articles from magazines and newspapers on social science, government, and scientific issues. Knowledge Source is the company's product that allows all the SIRS databases to be searched.
- SilverPlatter (*www.silverplatter.com/usa*). All of its databases are available on the Web through WebSPIRS.
- H. W. Wilson (*www.hwwilson.com*). Publisher of indexes on a wide range of subjects, with some full-text articles as well as other reference materials.

New companies have created products for the Web. For example, Dawson Information Quest, Inc., through Information Quest, provides bibliographic citations and tables of contents with links to CARL UnCover and the British Library for document delivery. More reference sources are being offered on the Web continually, and, the librarian can assume that most electronic reference resources will eventually be available also on the Web or even only on the Web. The Web will provide them with more flexibility to use multimedia, hypertext, and other enhancements as well as the ability to update rapidly.

REFERENCE SOURCES BY TYPE OF MATERIAL

Reference materials provide access to both current and retrospective information. There are many types of reference materials—including encyclopedias, dictionaries, directories, and atlases, indexes, and subject-specific reference works.

Many general reference books are available in several formats. The advantages and disadvantages of each format must be evaluated since the electronic versions do not necessarily add value to the reference work or make it easier to access. Sometimes, however, the reference work in both electronic and print format makes each more useful.

This section of the chapter highlights some of the new reference tools available in electronic formats and the additional value they offer to the librarian and user. It also points out reference materials that are equally valuable in print. The section begins by discussing types of reference materials such as encyclopedias and dictionaries, how the electronic capabilities have enhanced each type of reference source, and then gives examples of the reference sources available. It goes on to discuss the sciences, social sciences, and the humanities, pointing out the differences in scholarship in these areas and how they affect the development and use of electronic resources.

ENCYCLOPEDIAS

Encyclopedias present concise information on a large number of subjects. General encyclopedias provide information on all subjects; subject encyclopedias present information on all aspects of a subject. Encyclopedias provide quick, easy-to-use information in print; they adapt especially well to electronic formats for five reasons:

1. Hypertext allows users to move from one subject to related subjects with ease, and to find all the related material on a subject.
2. It is easier to keep all subjects up-to-date in an electronic format than in a print format. As a result, publishers of print encyclopedias recently have noted a drop in sales of the print versions of their product.[9]
3. The economics of printing and the popularity of the electronic versions are making it unfeasible to continue the print versions of encyclopedias.
4. Electronic formats more easily accommodate longer articles when appropriate.
5. Ease of updating and fact-checking material throughout means that there is more consistency in the electronic format than in the print.

The electronic format also permits encyclopedias to link to appropriate Web sites. They provide for simple searching as well as Boolean searching, and include illustrations, photographs, graphs, and maps.
Some of the disadvantages of electronic encyclopedias are:

1. The indexing guides the user to many articles that mention the subject or person being searched only in passing, and leads users to references far afield of the main subject. Users may spend a lot of time clicking on useless references.
2. Unless the library has a local area network, fewer people can use an electronic encyclopedia than can use a multivolume print set at the same time.

Among the most popular of the encyclopedias in print format are *The New Encyclopaedia Britannica, Encyclopedia Americana, Collier's*

Encyclopedia, World Book Encyclopedia, and *Compton's Encyclopedia.* Recent information makes it doubtful that the print versions of *Compton's* and *Collier's* will continue to be published.[10] All the encyclopedias are available on CD-ROMs, and most are now on the World Wide Web. Some are little more than the print format converted to an electronic format, but others have added a great deal of hypertext, sound, animation, and video.

- The *Microsoft Encarta Multimedia Encyclopedia,* based on the print *Funk & Wagnall's New Encyclopedia,* has the most sophisticated multimedia and is the oldest CD-ROM encyclopedia.
- *Encarta* has 30,000 articles, over 12,000 images, 70 videos, 1,350 audio clips, 450 charts and tables, 650 maps, and Web links. This new edition favors content over the multimedia features and has improved searching capability. It is an example of the greatly improved quality of reference works available on CD-ROM.
- The *Encyclopaedia Britannica,* known for its excellent articles, has developed links to the World Wide Web from its CD-ROM product. This enables users to considerably expand their research. Britannica has an online version of the encyclopedia and also has added a new Web directory called Britannica (*www. britannica. com*) that rates and reviews Web sites by subject.
- *Collier's Encyclopedia* is "a true multimedia encyclopedia on three discs with sound and movie clips, simulations, and links to the Internet."[11]
- *Compton's Interactive Encyclopedia* was the first true multimedia CD-ROM. It is user friendly, links to Web sites, and has monthly updates that can be downloaded from the Web.
- The Grolier Online Web site includes *Encyclopedia Americana,* the *Grolier Multimedia Encyclopedia Online,* and the *New Book of Knowledge Online.* Grolier Online provides information at three different levels. The *Encyclopedia Americana* has the most sophisticated information and offers in-depth reference that is more up-to-date than its print version. The *Grolier Multimedia Encyclopedia Online* is the electronic version of the *Academic American Encyclopedia* and offers a source of ready reference information. Finally, the *New Book of Knowledge Online* provides information at a level suitable for elementary school students.
- *World Book,* which produced a well-rated CD-ROM with a great deal of multimedia and good searching capability, has just introduced an online version.

- Generally regarded as a concise encyclopedia, the *Columbia Encyclopedia* is an excellent CD-ROM product. It has 51,000 entries and a well-designed screen.

Most libraries whose general encyclopedias are used extensively will want some in print as well as the electronic versions.

Specialized encyclopedias are a very useful resource on CD-ROM. A good example is the *Encyclopedia Judaica* that includes the 1972 text, the text of the yearbooks, and the decennial books from 1982 to 1992. Articles also have been updated, and photographs, film and audio clips, charts, and maps have been added. It was named one of *Library Journal*'s "Best Reference Sources 1997." Grove's *Dictionary of Art* is now available by subscription on the Web, and plans are in progress for an online version of the *New Grove Dictionary of Music and Musicians*.

DICTIONARIES, THESAURI, AND QUOTATION BOOKS

Dictionaries, thesauri, and quotation books are ready reference works that are easy to use in print format. Unabridged dictionaries attempt to be comprehensive and inclusive; *Webster's New International Dictionary*, the *Random House Dictionary of the English Language*, and the *Oxford English Dictionary* are the most popular. Abridged dictionaries in print format are more frequently used on a daily basis because they are smaller and easier to use. *The American Heritage Dictionary of the English Language, Random House Webster's College Dictionary, Merriam Webster's Collegiate Dictionary*, and *Webster's New World Dictionary of the English Language* are all well-rated, and they are also available on CD-ROM. Valuable features of electronic dictionaries include:

1. An audio capability so the user can hear the word pronounced.
2. Extensive search capacity. For example, the user can search for words that rhyme, for quotations by particular authors, for terms that came into use in a particular time period and for words of a particular ethnic origin.

Dictionaries also are available on the World Wide Web. In *The Wordsmyth English Dictionary-Thesaurus,* a new Web integrated dictionary-thesaurus, the user can look up a word once and get both the dictionary definition and hyperlinks to synonyms and other related words. This dictionary can be found at (*www/lightlink.com/bobp/wedt*). Another source on the Web is the Michigan Electronic Library collection of dictionaries at (*http://mel.lib.mi.us/reference/REF-dict.html*) that points to language dictionaries, thesauri, and other specialized dictionaries. Finally, OneLook Dictionaries (*www.onelook.com*) provides access to over 460 dictionaries, including both general and specialized dictionaries on a wide range of subjects from religion to science to technology.

Quotation books often are just as satisfactory in print format if the user simply wants to look up the author of a quotation or some other indexed information. However, quotation books have an increased search capacity in CD-ROM format. The user may be able to search by author or speaker's name, by keyword, alphabetically by quotations, and by combining terms such as century and nationality. For example, *The Columbia World of Quotations* on CD-ROM has 60,000 quotations (compared to 18,000 in the print version), and allows for both keyword and subject searching of more than 6,000 subject headings. The user also can perform author and speaker searches by nationality, occupation, gender, birth date, topic, or a combination of these possibilities. Another quotation book on CD-ROM is *Bartlett's Familiar Quotations*, which has 22,000 quotations; it allows searches by author, keyword, subject, date, and source; and uses the Boolean operators (AND and OR). Within the author search, the user can indicate gender, profession, and geographical location. Although *Bartlett's* is not as comprehensive as *Columbia*, it costs much less and includes author pictures, sound files, images of art, and video clips. It allows a great deal of flexibility in searching—by topic, author, date, keyword, source, and media—as well as by Boolean operators (AND and OR).

DIRECTORIES

Directories are an ideal reference work to transfer to CD-ROM or online because they need constant updating of information, such as names, addresses, phone numbers, and fax numbers. In an electronic format, the information can be changed rapidly so that the user will find the latest information. The searching capabilities also can be increased with an electronic format. In the print version only the most important fields are indexed; the electronic format allows searching of many fields. For example, *Associations Unlimited* is a five-part work of which three have print counterparts: "National Organizations of the U.S.," " International Organizations," and "Regional, State, and Local Organizations." The two parts new to the CD-ROM are "Association Materials," which includes the complete text of association membership categories and descriptive materials, and "Government Nonprofit," which has information on all organizations granted nonprofit status by the IRS. There are six search options: Search by Name, Search by Keyword, Search by Location, Extended Search, Search Nonprofit Organizations, and Expert Search. It is obvious that a great deal of additional searching can be done using the CD-ROM rather than the print version. This reference work is now also available by subscription through the Web.

Ulrich's International Periodicals Directory also is available on the Web. This valuable directory of 210,000 periodicals and serials can be searched simply by keyword or author. An advanced search strategy can be used to search other elements of the entries such as ISSN, publisher, indexing, and abstracting sources.

ATLASES

The visual aspects of atlases and maps lend themselves well to electronic formats. These new geographic products feature 3-D renderings, video clips, audio, Internet links, and the ability to zoom in and out.

The *Microsoft Encarta Virtual Globe* is an excellent product featuring many "bells and whistles" such as audio and video clips, Internet links, and interviews. Access is available through the country, a special topic, or through the directory of pictures and audio and video clips. In addition to the map of the country, the user can find statistical information and information on the land and climate, the culture and arts, the lifestyle and the society.

The Hammond Atlas of the World is one of the many CD-ROM geographic tools originally in print format. It has three sections: an atlas, an almanac, and thematics. Among its features are the ability to view two country maps side-by-side, and the ability to search for items such as airports, glaciers, Indian reservations. It also has a hypertext-linked almanac.

New Millennium World Atlas Deluxe CD-ROM provides clear and readable maps, including both city-center street maps and thematic maps. It also allows the user to compare two maps side by side.

Map 'n' Go is a CD-ROM product that allows the user to add a variety of specified sites such as bridges, universities, and even construction sites. It calculates routes quickly and provides annotations in the margins.

Among the excellent mapping products available on the Internet are:

- WebCrawler Map Thyself (*www.webcrawler.com/WebCrawler/FindAddress*), which allows users to type in an address anywhere in the United States and view a street map with the designated location highlighted. The user can zoom in for detail or zoom out to get information on the surrounding city or region. Produced by Geosys, which also produces MapQuest maps, WebCrawler provides a link to MapQuest for viewing points of interest in the surrounding area.

- MapQuest (*www.mapquest.com/*) has three options: interactive atlas, personalized maps, and TripQuest. Users can locate and map a variety of resources at a particular location, including foreign countries. After creating a map with MapQuest, the user can place a variety of icons on the map representing museums, schools, restaurants, recreational facilities, and the like. Driving directions are another component of MapQuest.
- Yahoo City Maps (*http://maps.yahoo.com/yahoo/*) and Lycos Road Maps (*www.lycos.com/roadmap.html*) both use Vicinity Corporation's maps for their databases. In both, the user can type in an address and then receive a map with the selected location marked by an X. Both provide driving directions.

Despite their value-added features, electronic atlases are not likely to replace print atlases. The clarity and color of the electronic maps do not meet the standards of the best of the print atlases. Web maps are good for routing maps and finding a particular location, but print atlases are far superior for details such as locating mountains, valleys, and rivers.

BIOGRAPHICAL SOURCE LOCATORS

Biographical and Genealogy Master Index, an index to over 200 publications, is one of the most comprehensive indexes for locating biographical information. This index is available on CD-ROM and is most useful in that format since it is a reference tool that can be checked quickly. The Biography Resource Center is a Web resource available by subscription containing 150,000 biographies and access to additional magazine and newspaper articles. Searches can be done by name, subject, nationality, place, and time.

Three free sources are also available.

1. Biographical Dictionary with its 24,000 entries can be found at (*www.s9.com/biography*). The information for each entry includes name, dates, and a short description of why the person is well known. The site can be searched by keyword to find awards, dates, discoveries and inventions, nationalities, professions, and more. There are links to other sites with lists of famous people such as astronauts, Nobel Prize winners, and politicians.

2. Biography, produced by A&E Television, is another Web site for biographical information (*www.biography.com*). This has a slightly smaller number of entries (about 20,000), but it provides more information than Biographical Dictionary. This Web site also links to other biography-related sites.

3. The World Biographical Index (*www.biblio.tu-bs.de/allegro/*) has access to 2.8 million biographical articles on 1.7 million individuals. Information covers pseudonyms, dates, occupations, and subjects' locations within the biographical archive published by K. G. Saur Publishing Co.; it also has links to related Web sites.

GOVERNMENT INFORMATION SOURCES

A great deal of government information, from *Statistical Abstracts of the United States* to *Country Handbooks*, is available in electronic format, and much of it is on the World Wide Web. The government plans to convert everything to electronic format, keeping only twenty-four core titles available in print.

Of particular interest is the Web access to the *Monthly Catalog of U.S. Government Publications* (*www.access.gpo.gov/su_docs/dpos/adpos400.html*), which provides an easy way to check for particular titles or subjects. Other valuable government sources available through GPO Access (*www.access.gpo.gov/su_docs*) are the *Code of Federal Regulations*, the *Congressional Record*, the *Federal Record*, and the *U.S. Code*. In print, these publications take up an enormous amount of space in libraries and have to be searched volume by volume. Their Web counterparts are a welcome change.

A good example of a useful government information source available on the Internet is the U.S. Census. Much of the information is available at no charge. The homepage of the Bureau of the Census includes full texts of selected census reports and data tables, press releases, and related information (*www.census.gov*). The site can be searched by subject or by free-text search. To access databases that are maintained by the Census Bureau but that are not part of their publications, the user must subscribe to CenStats.

Another useful census tool is *CensusCD + Maps*, which has the entire 1990 census of Population and Housing on one CD-ROM disc. It enables the user to formulate a customized search. Information down to the block-group level is included. There are also 1997 estimates and 2002 projections for block groups, tracts, zip codes, counties, and states.

Federal statistics are available through FedStats(*www.fedstats.gov)*, a site maintained by the Federal Interagency Council on Statistical Policy that offers information from over 70 federal agencies. Some of the information comes from the *Statistical Abstract of the United States*, and other statistics are derived directly from the agencies.

INDEXES

Electronic technology has affected indexes more than any other type of reference source. Print indexes have always been slow to arrive and required searching through a number of volumes in order to identify relevant articles. Electronic indexes are produced more rapidly and integrate all the volumes into one, with the entries arranged by date. Beyond this, the searching capability has been greatly enhanced. Depending on the database, keyword and Boolean searching usually are available. With one search, users can bring up a tremendous number of citations of articles and find an abstract and possibly the full text of the article. Full text may be available through the database itself, through an online link, through document delivery, or through interlibrary loan. Full text is often plain, unformatted text (an ASCII file), but a few publishers offer some image files that provide the look of the original journal or newspaper (such as Bell & Howell Information & Learning's *ProQuest Direct* and Information Access Company's *SearchBank*).

Although these indexes often seem like a dream come true, many problems need to be resolved. For example, often the complete periodical is not available in full, sometimes omitting letters, editorials, book reviews, and short news articles. Many do not reproduce the graphics (tables, graphs, etc.), or else reproduce them poorly.[12] In addition, the full text of some periodicals is withheld for a period of time before being released to the database at the request of the publisher.

The following checklist can be used in evaluating periodical indexes:

- number of titles indexed and abstracted
- number of titles in full text
- number of titles in full image
- back files available
- newspaper titles in full text
- access by periodical title available
- quality of abstracts
- quality of indexing
- currency of updates
- response time to reach data (if on the Web)
- quality of user documentation provided
- statistics produced
- full printing and downloading rights available
- ability to e-mail or fax articles to users
- price

There are four main publishers in the index field:

1. Bell & Howell Information & Learning (formerly UMI)
2. IAC (Information Access Company, part of The Gale Group)
3. EBSCO
4. H. W. Wilson

Each of these companies has developed a number of products to fit different niches in the market. There are indexes for different types of libraries such as public, school, and academic libraries. There are indexes on CD-ROM, ones that are commercial online, and ones that can be locally tape-loaded by the library. Now there are also indexes accessible through the Internet/World Wide Web.

IAC (Information Access Company) was an early entrant into the electronic publishing arena, and it continues to hold a prominent place in the industry. It provides its databases—both bibliographic and full text—on CD-ROM, online, and through the Web. IAC has many periodical database products designed to fit the needs of different libraries. Some of its databases are accessible through Dialog and through LEXIS-NEXIS.

Bell & Howell Information & Learning began as a supplier of microforms to libraries. This company has now expanded into bibliographic databases and full text on CD-ROM, online, and on the World Wide Web. Bell & Howell has acquired DataTimes, a supplier of full-text regional newspaper and business databases. It also has entered into an agreement with H. W. Wilson to combine Wilson's bibliographic databases with Bell & Howell's full-text databases. They will appear first on CD-ROM and then on ProQuest Direct.

H. W. Wilson, a producer of print periodical indexes for many years, has been a slow entrant into the electronic reference field. It offers access to its indexes on the World Wide Web as well as on CD-ROM and online.

EBSCO began as a periodical vendor and then made its entry into the periodical index field. It also provides access to its indexes on CD-ROM, online, and on the Web, and provides a great deal of full text.

A new entrant into the world of Web indexes is Softline Information, Inc., which has produced three indexes first on CD-ROM and now on the Net. They are *Ethnic NewsWatch*, a source of full-text articles in English and Spanish from ethnic and minority publications, *GenderWatch*, a source of full-text articles on women's and gender issues, and *Alt•HealthWatch*, a source of full-text articles on alternative and complementary approaches to healthcare and wellness.

Searching ease varies a great deal from index to index, and libraries are finding that users are not yet comfortable with electronic access only. They often want the option of both the print and electronic versions for the full text of a journal article. This presents complex and expensive problems for institutions hoping to save space and funding by switching to electronic formats.

REFERENCE SOURCES BY SUBJECT

THE SCIENCES

The sciences were early users of electronic products. The need for up-to-date information in the sciences has made electronic resources particularly valuable, since, by the time science information is in print, it is dated and often superseded. Scientists are accustomed to scanning tables of contents and picking out articles of interest to them—something that is feasible with electronic databases.

A study of the user acceptance of electronic journals conducted by Linda Stewart at Cornell University revealed the features judged most important by a group of faculty and graduate students from the chemistry department. These features in priority order were:

- ability to create a print copy
- ability to browse graphics to determine the value of an article
- ability to browse text to keep current with related research and to generate new ideas
- portability of the text
- ability to underline and annotate
- ability to flip and scan pages
- adequate type font
- text design and layout
- physical comfort

"At least 84 percent or more of the respondents considered electronic journals capable of satisfying the need for adequate type fonts, browsing text and graphics, and underlining and annotating."[13] Another study (by Ann Peterson Bishop[14]) asked "Could electronic journals be used for all scholarly journal reading?" and found that users want and need a print copy, something that is permanent, portable, and easy to read, and that they don't like the instability of electronic information.

Basic Sources

The basic reference work in the sciences is the *McGraw-Hill Encyclopedia of Science and Technology*, available on CD-ROM and in print. It is useful for a wide range of users of public and academic libraries. Plans are for this valuable work to be available online in the near future. Another basic reference tool is the *Academic Press Dictionary of Science and Technology*. This is now available on CD-ROM at a lower cost than the print version. Enhancements to the print version include spoken pronunciation for 3,500 difficult terms and new color illustrations. Searching can be done by keyword and Boolean. *Elements Explorer: A Multimedia Guide to the Periodic Table* on CD-ROM provides a wealth of information about each element including the atomic number, atomic symbol, melting point, and boiling point. There are also hyperlinks to articles containing additional information.

Many good Web sites for the sciences have been developed. The Math & Science Gateway (*www.tc.cornell.edu/Edu/MathSciGateway*) was developed at Cornell University for teachers and students grades 9 through 12, but it is also recommended for adults. The Nine Planets (*http://seds.lpl.arizona.edu/nineplanets/nineplanets/nineplanets.html*) provides information on the history, mythology, and science of the solar system. Finally, Geology and the Environment (*www.hic.net/hicpersonal/j/jbutler/update/cit.htm*) covers all aspects of geology.

In medicine, electronic access to information has been useful to both the scientist and the layperson. Medical handbooks have been very successful on CD-ROM. Two good examples are *American Medical Association Family Medical Guide* and *Mayo Clinic Family Health*. On the Net, the National Library of Medicine's PubMed provides free access to Medline. Through Medline the user can obtain citations and abstracts as well as related articles. For scientists, being able to keep up with the latest medical information has greatly enhanced their ability to move research forward in a timely manner.

Advanced Sources

The following are major players in the production of electronic products in the sciences:

- Chemical Abstracts Service is the producer of *Chemical Abstracts*, a major bibliographic source in the field of chemistry. This company also has become a database distributor.
- STN International, which is a cooperative venture with companies in Germany and Japan, provides access to over 200 bibliographic, directory, and full-text databases. STN also offers many Web-based products.

- Ovid Technologies, Inc., specializes in science, technology, and medical databases—both bibliographic and full text. Ovid offers products on CD-ROM, online, and on the Web.
- Questal-Orbit, Inc., delivers information online. It offers many standard bibliographical databases and some specialized ones in the areas of science and technology.

The Internet is another useful resource for the sciences:

- ScienceDirect (Elsevier Science) is a new Web product that provides access to most of Elsevier's science journals (1997–present). Many libraries will find it too costly, however, unless reasonable consortial arrangements can be negotiated.
- The American Mathematical Society has developed MathSciNet, a Web subscription database that includes *Mathematical Reviews* and *Current Mathematical Publications*, two of the society's publications. They are available online through Dialog and the World Wide Web.
- For statistics, Carnegie-Mellon University has developed Statlib (*www.stat.cmu.edu/*), which gathers together in one site statistics from many different disciplines both in the sciences and social sciences.

THE SOCIAL SCIENCES

The social sciences are slowly beginning to embrace electronic formats. Social scientists use journal articles and rely on citations in journal articles as a way to expand their research, which can run the gamut from historical texts to current literature. They often do not rely on traditional library bibliographic tools such as indexes. However, as the sources of electronic information in the social sciences increase, it will be up to librarians to introduce them to their users.

Basic Sources

A great deal of information in political science is available on CD-ROM and on the Web. *Facts On File World News*, on CD-ROM, includes all the information published in *Facts On File* from 1980 to the present. Updated quarterly, searches can be done by keyword or by subject, and hyperlinks connect the various aspects of a story. *CQ.Com on Congress* (Congressional Quarterly) publishes *CQ Weekly*, *CQ Researcher*, and the *Daily Monitor*, where users can find information and analysis on all aspects of Congress from bills and legislative summaries to reports on congressional committees and profiles of members of Congress. An example of a free Web site is Project Vote Smart (*www.vote-smart.org)*, which contains information about politicians free of charge. There are three parts to this site: (1) Candidates and Elected Officials has biographical information, issue positions, campaign finance information, voting records, and performance evaluations from special groups; (2) CongressTrack tracks voting records and the status of legislation; and (3) Government and Politics includes information on state governments, voter registration information, and legislative district maps.

Newspaper access has greatly improved due to the Internet. Most libraries often could afford to buy only a few newspapers on microfilm, and many only subscribed to the *New York Times*. Now with Internet access, researchers can access many more newspapers. Some are free, and some require a subscription:

- The *Christian Science Monitor* (*www.csmonitor.com/*) is available free on the Internet. Its archives go back to 1980, although they are not complete; nevertheless, it is an excellent research tool for the social scientist, especially for international articles.
- The *Washington Post* (*www.washingtonpost.com/wp-srv/searches/mainsrch.htm*) currently archives only two weeks of back issues. The full-text archives will be extended back to 1986. Other sources of the *Washington Post* are Dialog, with indexing and full text back to May 1983, and NEXIS, with full text of the *Post* from January 1977 to the present. The *Washington Post* is particularly useful to social scientists researching governmental news.

The Internet has been a boon to the business world. Information, especially on finance and the financial markets, has exploded as a result of the Internet. Individuals now research stocks on their own and buy them through the Internet. All the major search engines provide extensive free information on stocks on their sites. Although there are many fee-based sources of information such as *Value Line*, there is so much free information that the average person doesn't even consider paying. The major index companies also provide business indexes such as Bell & Howell's *ABI Inform*, IAC's *General Business File ASAP*, and EBSCO's *Business Source Elite*. Many business directories are available either on CD-ROM or the Web. For example, there is *Import/Export USA*, which is issued monthly and provides government information on over 20,000 commodities for more than 200 countries. The user can determine who exports certain commodities and who imports them. Reference USA (InfoUSA) is a Web database of 10.5 million businesses. Searches can be done by company, geography, type of business, and business size. Searches can be narrowed by selecting from a long list of possible criteria. For libraries preferring

CD-ROMs, *The American Business Disc* provides information on 10 million businesses on one disc. There are also government business Web sites such as the Small Business Administration site (*www.sba. gov*), which includes forms and publications, laws and regulations, and loan and financing information, as well as online courses and Great Business Hotlinks, which links the user to other public and private business sites.

Advanced Sources

Contemporary Women's Issues is a full-text CD-ROM that indexes journals as well as other literature such as research reports and newsletters. It covers more than 600 international resources since 1992, with quarterly updates. There are also many sources of women's history materials on the Internet. These include the Library of Congress's site, which focuses on U.S. women's suffrage campaigns (*http:// lcweb2.loc.gov/ammem/vfwhtml/vfwhome.html*), and Duke University's Special Collections Library, which has digitized documents from the Women's Liberation Movement of the late 1960s and early 1970s (*http://scriptorium.lib.duke.edu/wim/*).

Current Issues Sourcefile gives the full texts of position papers and other special reports from a wide variety of organizations on ten major subject areas: business and economics, crime, environment, education, health, government, international issues, science and technology, population, and social issues. Searching can be done by subject, keyword, and source. This CD-ROM provides a wealth of information from sources not easily available.

An online database available through LEXIS-NEXIS is Congressional Universe, which combines the CIS/Index with the LEXIS-NEXIS database on congressional legislation. Although this information is available less expensively through GPO Access and Thomas, this product provides excellent indexing and more full text, including bills, laws, hearings, and other congressional documents.

Moody's Company Data Direct is a Web-accessible database with information on over 10,000 U.S.-based public companies. It provides weekly updated company information, company financial reports, SEC filings, real-time news headlines and complete text, and the usual directory type of information.

The Andrew Mellon Foundation has funded JSTOR, an important project that includes many journals in the social sciences. This project is converting back issues of over one hundred scholarly journals at least five years old in the fields of economics, history, mathematics, political science, anthropology, sociology, and more, into electronic form so they can continue to be accessible without institutions having to preserve the print copies. Each journal has a text version, an image version, and an index. In its first phase (to end in 1999), JSTOR has 116 journals. More than 350 libraries from the United States, Canada, and Great Britain are participating in this project. The first participants were academic libraries, but other types of libraries are projected to join in.

THE HUMANITIES

The humanities has been slow to adopt electronic technology, having always been a field that relied upon the printed word and embracing the whole array of printed materials from the beginning of print, rather than concentrating on current information. The book as a physical object intertwined with the intellectual content has been the source of study for scholars in the humanities. Since humanists rely as much (if not more) on monographs than on journal articles, it is not surprising to find many full-length books being digitized. People working in the humanities use a wide variety of materials including book reviews and publishers' catalogs and depend heavily on browsing, footnotes, and consulting with colleagues.

The vocabulary of some of the disciplines in the humanities is less precise than that of the sciences and social sciences, so it becomes more difficult to use the traditional selection of index terms for bibliographic retrieval. There also is a heavy reliance on proper terms/names. Humanities scholars need indexes with an enriched vocabulary and the ability to search by genre, literary period, location, and literary technique. Hypertext has a good potential in the humanities by linking terms, icons, images, and sounds among related documents. Examples of hypermedia projects are *Project Perseus*, a CD-ROM product on Greek literature, and the products made available through the World Wide Web from the Institute for Advanced Technology in the Humanities at the University of Virginia that include the British Poetry Archive, the Dante Gabriel Rossetti Archive, the Pompeii Archive and the Civil War Archive.

Of interest to humanities scholars are electronic text files, library catalogs with primary source material, e-journals, full-text databases, Web sites on particular writers and artists, and full texts of secondary literature such as literary criticism.

- Project Gutenberg (*www.promo.net/pg/*) is one of the oldest digital projects; its goal is to make novels, short stories, reference works, and other informational texts available on the Internet. The texts are produced in ASCII to make them as accessible as possible.
- A similar project is the Oxford Text Archive (OTA) (*http://info.ox.ac.uk/~archive/ota.html*), which stores and maintains the

electronic texts of scholars but also stores the text of literary works and some reference books. There are also many electronic sites devoted to the work of one author that often include not only the author's actual texts but also applicable reference works. Some of the authors with separate sites are Jane Austen, William Shakespeare, F. Scott Fitzgerald, James Joyce, J.R.R. Tolkien, Jack London, and Mark Twain. There are also several sites that have linguistics resources.

- A third site is the Berkeley Digital Library SunSITE, which has among its resources the Emma Goldman Papers, the Jack London Collection, Literature (it is increasing title by title), and the Online Medieval and Classical Library (also adding material title by title).

Although the proliferation of electronic resources in the humanities will, no doubt, encourage electronic research, the attraction of the humanist for the book and journal article and for the use of primary source materials will remain an important source of research. For many, it may simply be that there is not yet a critical mass of material in electronic format.

Basic Sources

In literature, a variety of reference titles are now available electronically. A popular title is *Masterplots Complete CD-ROM*, which combines the full text of the entire 80-volume series on one disc. This format has the advantage of being easy to search, is well priced, and prevents users from being tempted to steal a page or two since they can print the pages they want. Another CD-ROM product is the electronic version of *Romeo and Juliet*. Although expensive, it has some excellent features about characters and their interrelationships that can be clicked on at any point if the reader becomes confused, and the translation of Elizabethan terms into modern English. This is a fine example of a research product providing coverage of a specialized subject area. It was named as one of *Library Journal*'s "Best Reference Sources 1997." A similar disc is available for *Macbeth*.

Two new CD-ROM products offer easy access to historical documents. *Landmark Documents in American History* comprises more than 1,200 documents ranging from speeches, Supreme Court decisions, treaties, and acts to letters, amendments, and legislation. These documents contain photos, videos, and other illustrations. Indexing allows searching by time period, subject, person, or keyword. *Scribner's American History and Culture* contains more than 8,000 articles on American political, economic, and social issues. Full-text articles come from a number of well-known reference books including *The Dictio-*

nary of American History and *The Dictionary of American Biography*. The articles are linked to photographs.

For philosophy, there is a CD-ROM version of the *Routledge Encyclopedia of Philosophy* that provides the user access by time period, individual philosopher, philosophical issues and theories, and terminology. A flexible search engine allows the user to manipulate the database.

A useful art resource is to be found on the World Wide Web. World Wide Art Resources (WWAR) (*http://wwar.com*) provides both images from the work of artists and links to art resources including museums and exhibitions, festivals, art education, art publications, and even employment and art supplies. The site's search engine accesses specific resources needed by the users.

Advanced Sources

Commercial online databases include databases of interest to humanities scholars. On Dialog there are databases in the areas of architecture, arts, humanities, language and linguistics, philosophy, and religion. On RLIN (Research Libraries Information Network) there are several databases of interest to humanists including *Avery Index to Architectural Periodicals*, *The Eighteenth Century Short Title Catalogue*, and *SPIPIO*, the art sales catalog database.

Art CD-ROMs are being published that provide useful and unique resources. For example, *RM* is an overview of the work of Robert Mapplethorpe, with 450 images and video interviews with the artist and others. All images are indexed so they can be searched, and are zoomable. A less contemporary example is *Leonardo da Vinci*, which presents a biography of the artist, an essay on the Renaissance, narratives and analyses of topics addressed in his *Codex Leicester*, and copies of paintings, drawings, and manuscripts.

In literature, the *MLA Bibliography*, an index to critical material on literature, drama, languages, linguistics, and folklore, is now on the Web. *Literature Online* (LION), a product of Chadwyck-Healey, provides World Wide Web access to the full texts of more than 205,000 English and American poems, novels, and plays from 600 A.D. to the present, and to reference works such as dictionaries and bibliographies; there is a master index to the complete database. Much of the literature on LION is out-of-print. Among the reference works are *The Annual Bibliography of English Language and Literature (ABELL)* and the *Bibliography of American Literature*. This company's latest product is the *International Index to the Performing Arts*, devoted to performing arts periodicals. Chadwyck-Healey has also produced collections on CD-ROM including Afro-American Poetry, the complete poetical works of English and American poets, early American fiction, and nineteenth-century fiction.

In the field of history there is *IDIOM History*, which lists the MARC records, the tables of contents, and back-of-the-book indexes of 2,500 monographs. This arrangement allows researchers to find specific information that would not be evident by looking at the tables of contents of the books.

TOOLS FOR DEVELOPING REFERENCE COLLECTIONS

This part of the chapter emphasizes other tools available to evaluate electronic resources. The most frequently used review sources for print materials are *Library Journal, Kirkus, Booklist, School Library Journal* (used by public and school libraries), *Publishers Weekly* (used mainly by public libraries), and *Choice* (used by large public libraries and academic libraries). *Library Journal* has separate columns reviewing a selective number of CD-ROMs and Web sites. Carol Tenopir's column is an excellent source for what is happening in the technology field. "LJ INFOTECH Online Databases" also is well worth reading regularly to keep abreast of the present and future trends. "Databases & Disc Reviews" by Cheryl LaGuardia reviews both new databases and new CD-ROM titles. LaGuardia provides a summary of each product—the subject matter, how it compares to the print version if one exists, special audio and video features, and how well the search engine works. The "Bottom Line" indicates if the item is recommended or not. *School Library Journal* has a CD-ROM and Software review column that reviews the strengths, weaknesses, and uses of each product. *Choice* integrates all reviews of electronic formats (such as CD-ROMs and Web sites) in the appropriate subject area. *Booklist* reviews reference materials in electronic formats as part of their "Subscription Books Bulletin" section.

In addition to these periodicals, the *Reference & User Services Quarterly*, published by the ALA Reference and User Services Section, has a "Databases" column by David Kohl that reviews electronic resources in all formats. *Software and CD-ROM Reviews On File, Monthly Survey of Computer Software and CD-ROM Reviews* provides a product description and analysis as well as a list of reviews of each product. One section is devoted to reference material.

The major problem for electronic reference materials is that reviewing is much more selective and slower than the reviewing of print materials, so librarians should look for reviews elsewhere. For example, the *New York Times* reviews electronic products every Thursday in its "Circuits" section, and other newspapers review CD-ROMs and Internet sites.

Recent books on CD-ROM include:

- *The Multimedia and CD-ROM Directory on CD-ROM*, which provides access to more than 16,000 CD-ROM titles and 13,000 CD-ROM companies; users can search by whole record, title, ISBN, publisher, information provider, subject, type of data, date of current issue, language, computer, operating system, software, network, software producer, price, and disc manufacturer.
- *CD-ROM for Librarians and Educators: A Guide to Over 800 Instructional Resources* is another guide to CD-ROMs that support typical curricular areas.

In *Computers in Libraries*, Paul Nicholls writes a short column, "CD-ROM Librarian," about CD-ROMs that is followed by a news section on new CD-ROM products. The listings are informative but give no evaluation. There is also a feature article on CD-ROMs in each issue.

INTERNET DIRECTORIES AND EVALUATIVE GUIDES

Many search engines and directories on the Internet review Web sites and compile their own lists of the best.

- Lycos Top 5% (*http://point.lycos.com/categories*) is the oldest Web site directory. Each site selected gets a detailed review describing its editorial and visual merits. There are three rating categories: content, design, and overall. The user can sort the listings by any of the three rating categories to see which sites rank the highest in any one of 18 fields. Listings can be sorted by topic, and within that by review date.
- Magellan Internet Guide (*www.mckinley.com/*), owned by Excite, Inc., describes and reviews and rates Internet resources. This very large international database reviews English, French, and German sites.
- Yahoo (*www.yahoo.com/*) catalogs sites manually, often based on user recommendations. Although it has many quality sites, it does not screen sites according to any specific criteria. The sites are divided into 14 broad subject areas and then subdivided into smaller categories.
- Argus Clearinghouse (*www.clearinghouse.net/*) recommends

Web sites based on specific criteria including content, quality, design, and organization. There are topical guides for 13 subject areas ranging from health and medicine to arts and entertainment that are evaluated, rated, and indexed by category. They can be searched by keywords, titles, and authors.

- The Scout Report (*scout.cs.wisc.edu/scout/index.html*), housed in the Computer Science Department of the University of Wisconsin, is published every Friday and lists new Web sites that meet the report's criteria. The criteria for inclusion are content, authority, information maintenance (as in regular updating), presentation, availability (of the site and the links that can be reached), and cost. Although this is not a site developed by librarians, library-like criteria are used for selection.

There are regular reviews of Web sites in certain periodicals. *Library Journal* reviews new Web sites in "WebWatch." The reviews are often thematic, looking at sites such as ones on senior citizens or on environmental issues. Each site is described and evaluated and the developers identified. All aspects of the site are discussed, from layout to content. Finally the pros and cons of the site are listed and a "Bottom Line" recommendation given. In *Computers in Libraries*, Laverna Saunders writes the "Internet Librarian," which includes a short column, a news section, and a feature article on the Internet. Web database reviews can also be found in the "Reference Books Bulletin" section of *Booklist*, and in the magazines *Online* and *Database*.

There are several good directories that can be consulted to get information on databases on the Web. *Gale Directory of Databases* tells where to search a particular subject, as does *Net.Journal Directory*, which lists 9,500 journal titles available online and 700 Web archives and newspaper titles. *Fulltext Sources* lists sources of full texts online, and the *Directory of Electronic Journals, Newsletters and Academic Discussion Lists* (*http://arl.cni.org/scomm/edir/index.html*) describes and links to about 1,700 entries

Another resource is *Evaluating Internet Web Sites: An Educator's Guide* by Kathy Schrock, which gives 36 criteria for teachers to use in evaluating Web sites. Hope Tillman's "Evaluating Quality on the Net" (*www.tiac.net/users/hope/find.qual.html*) includes a great deal of valuable information on every aspect of the Internet. "Scholarly Electronic Publishing" is a bibliography published by Charles W. Bailey, Jr., Assistant Dean for Systems, University Libraries, University of Houston (TX), that "presents over 600 articles, books, electronic documents, and other sources that are useful in understanding scholarly electronic publishing efforts on the Internet and other networks." (*http://info.lib.uh.edu/sepb/sepb.html*)

New electronic information resources will continue to be published, but keeping up with them will not be easy since the number of reviews is still quite small. Library conference exhibits as well as the traditional library reviewing media are places to start. More reviewing media will no doubt appear in the next few years as libraries buy more electronic resources and need evaluations of them.

NOTES

1. Suzanne Mantel, "Looking It Up Is Looking Up." *Publishers Weekly* (September 29, 1997): 51.
2. Walt Crawford, "Paper Persists: Why Physical Library Collections Still Matter." *Online* (January 1998) *www.onlineinc.com*
3. "CD-ROM Review." *Library Journal* (November 15, 1996): 96.
4. "CD-ROM Review." *Library Journal* (June 15, 1997): 107.
5. Reference Announcement Issue. *Library Journal* (November 15, 1998): S3.
6. Chuck Koutnik, "The World Wide Web Is Here: Is the End of Printed Reference Sources Near?" *RQ* (Spring 1997): 422–425.
7. Joelle Klein, "Duke Study: Users at Library for Net," *Library Journal* (May 1, 1998): 14.
8. Norman Oder, "Cataloging the Net: Can We Do It," *Library Journal* (October 1, 1998): 47–51.
9. Mary Ellen Quinn. "Encyclopedia Update, 1997." *Booklist* (September 15, 1997): 251.
10. "Encyclopedia Update, 1998." *Booklist* (September 15, 1998): 251.
11. "Electronic Encyclopedia Update," *Booklist* (November 1, 1997):
12. Carol Franck and Holly Chambers, "How Full is the Full in Full-Text?" Poster Session, American Library Association Conference, June 27, 1998.
13. Linda Stewart, "User Acceptance of Electronic Journals: Interviews with Chemists at Cornell University," *College and Research Libraries* (July 1996): 342.
14. Stewart: 345.

2 CHANGING REFERENCE SERVICE PATTERNS AND MODELS

Reference service has long been thought of as a face-to-face transaction performed by a librarian at a reference desk. In practice, however, this service has little relationship to the desk and in actuality has no boundaries and can be performed in a myriad of locations. It has often been described as human mediation or as the ability to analyze a research question, apply critical thinking skills to the question, and use information resources through a knowledge of how information is organized to find the answer. The reference transaction connects resources to the interaction of the user and the librarian. As librarians have rethought the reference transaction and in some cases divided it into a series of transactions, reference service has begun to change.

This need to rethink the reference transaction has come about largely due to the new technology. In addition to an already busy reference desk, librarians have to deal with teaching users how to use the new technology (both hardware and software) and with having to learn the new technologies and databases themselves. They also have been faced with troubleshooting problems with hardware and software and dealing with the many issues the new technology has produced, such as space for workstations, which formats to use, and how to allocate staffing.

This chapter discusses some of the new, emerging patterns of reference service—both within the library and for remote users. Within the library, new models are being developed to handle better the increased business in the reference room that now includes user requests both for information and for assistance with the new electronic databases. Models for both public libraries and academic libraries also are examined. Since many users cannot or are not willing to come to the library for reference assistance, models for reference service by phone and e-mail are discussed as well as the use of synchronous (real-time) electronic reference that have made it possible to request and receive reference service remotely. These new technological mediums are examined as to how they function and how they can be structured to work effectively.

With the changes in reference service, libraries have begun to experiment with different staffing models. Although this change had already begun to take place in some libraries, the additional electronic reference tools have put an increasingly heavy burden on librarians and forced them to develop alternative models. Among the issues to be addressed as new models evolve are what services will be provided, the location of the service(s), and the staffing pattern. Librarians have also broken down the needs of the user and developed services to address each need. User needs fall into: directional information and other kinds of general information about the library; technical assistance using computers to access online public access catalogs, databases, and the Internet; ready reference assistance; in-depth reference assistance; and user instruction.

IN-LIBRARY REFERENCE SERVICE

ACADEMIC LIBRARY MODELS

The reference service pioneered by Virginia Massey-Burzio, first at Brandeis University and then at Johns Hopkins University, is a two-level reference service often called the "research consultation model":

1. The first level of service is staffed by graduate students (who are trained by the librarians) who answer basic, often repetitive directional and ready reference questions and refer the more difficult questions to librarians.
2. The second level of service is staffed by librarians who work one-on-one with those users who have the more extensive reference needs.

This model not only frees the librarian to spend a concentrated period of time with the user but also encourages a relationship between the librarian and user in which the user will want to make follow-up appointments for more assistance. In an evaluation of this project, Douglas Herman noted that it was difficult to train information desk staff so that they could distinguish questions that needed to be referred. Among his recommendations were: have a complete and reliable local catalog; train information desk staff to evaluate the questions, and not on knowledge of reference materials; and have ongoing training of information desk staff.[1]

At Rutgers University, a model was developed with three levels of service that is often referred to as "tiered reference service."

1. The first level needs minimum human intervention and includes the development of various ways for the students to help themselves through better signage, better maps of the li-

brary, a printed guide to library resources, guides to resources in various subject areas, computer-assisted instruction, and computerized information kiosks.

2. At the second level, trained paraprofessionals and library interns assist the users in basic bibliographic instruction and library orientation, directional information, ready reference, bibliographic verification (on OCLC, RLIN, and the online catalog), assistance with search strategies, basic informational services with referrals as needed, and technical assistance with machine problems.

3. At the third level, librarians and subject specialists provide individualized, in-depth research assistance, specialized reference services, specialized bibliographic instruction, mediated online searching, and liaison work with academic departments. The library also has experimented with various ways to work with faculty and their departments, communicating with them through listserv software and newsletters as well as by attending faculty meetings. Level three may even involve a librarian being on hand when a faculty member meets with a student to provide assistance with research projects.[2]

The University of Arizona Library has implemented a similar tiered system.

1. The first level is the information desk, which handles directional and other basic questions and is staffed by career staff and students.

2. The second level deals with the kinds of questions traditionally handled by a reference desk and is staffed by librarians, career staff, and library school students.

3. The third level is an appointments-only, one-to-one reference service staffed by librarians.[3]

Librarians at the Sterling C. Evans Library at Texas A&M developed a different tiered reference service.

1. The first level of service is the general information desk, staffed primarily by nonlibrarians, who provide directions and basic information about the online catalog and the electronic databases.

2. The second level is the reference desk. Both librarians and support staff work at this desk, assisting users with more in-depth research and with various reference tools.

3. The third level in this library is the database room, staffed by librarians, other staff, and students who are all well trained

in the use of the various databases available. The students help with the equipment and answer basic questions, and the rest of the staff assists the users to structure database searches, select appropriate databases, and search online. Referrals to the database room are often made from the reference desk.

Other libraries such as Michigan State University and the University of California, San Diego, have placed information desks staffed by nonlibrarians at the entrances to their libraries to answer basic information questions and to provide directions and referrals. By eliminating these quickly answered questions, the librarians at the reference desk have more time to work with users with more extensive needs.

PUBLIC LIBRARY MODELS

Academic libraries are not the only organizations trying new models of reference service. Alternative models are being developed also by public libraries, although their efforts have not been as well documented in the literature. The Harford County Public Library (MD) has created information stations in two or three locations scattered throughout the adult area instead of having a single reference desk. The theory behind this arrangement is that users are often looking for materials and information but do not bother to go to the reference desk because it is not close by. By having information stations closer to the users, there is more access to a librarian. Each station has a desk, chair, computer workstation, and ready reference tools.[4]

The Skokie Public Library (IL) has hired "Roving Technology Guides" who are equipped with pagers so they can be notified of users with problems. The Guides assist people in using the electronic workstation and those having technical problems. The Queens Borough Public Library (NY) uses high-school-aged, part-time staff called "Teen 'Net Mentors" to assist the public in the use of computers. These Mentors offer one-to-one assistance to library patrons in computer terminal usage, the Library's OPAC, and the Internet.

As public librarians have had new tasks added to their responsibilities, they have begun to delegate some of their duties. Many libraries have established an information desk at the entrance to the library staffed by nonlibrarians or even volunteers to answer simple informational and directional questions. Other public libraries are developing a special desk staffed by nonlibrarians where users can check out reference materials such as investment resources and sign up for the Internet and other computer workstations. All of this relieves the librarians so they can concentrate more on reference inquiries and less on tasks that don't require their skills. Expect to see public librarians move away from their reference desks in the next few years to meet with local community agencies and businesses that need assistance in finding information. They will, no doubt, move into more active consultation roles, reaching out to their users and communicating with them by electronic means.

STAFFING PATTERNS

Tiered reference services require deploying staff in a tiered manner. Paraprofessionals or students handle basic reference services, which necessitates ongoing training in order to maintain a quality service. It is particularly important to train staff to distinguish when to refer questions to a librarian. There is a natural tendency of staff to want to help the user no matter the level of the questions, so staff need to understand what each level of the service should do. This includes the difference between the responsibilities of librarians and paraprofessionals and, at the other end of the spectrum, the difference between those of the paraprofessionals and the clerical staff.

Many university libraries have actively been working to determine how faculty and graduate students conduct research in an effort to improve the service librarians render. Librarians are taking a proactive stance, offering specialized seminars and instructional sessions for students and faculty in specific departments, and even establishing office hours in an academic department. They spend more of their time advising students and faculty about how to do their research and how to develop their searches. The need for librarians who are subject specialists is paramount in these new roles. They must learn the new electronic tools and keep up-to-date. Libraries such as the one at Rutgers University have gone further, holding focus groups, conducting interviews, and distributing surveys to obtain more detailed information as to how faculty and students use library materials, especially the electronic databases.

Finally, some libraries have assigned librarians to both ready reference and more in-depth assistance. When librarians doing ready reference identify someone in need of more in-depth assistance, they offer to make an appointment so that more time can be spent with the user. Libraries using this model feel that it is important that librarians continue to work at both levels of reference service so as to keep the librarian in touch with user needs. They also believe that it is important to recognize that the first level of reference service is a way to get people started and to identify users who will need additional assistance.

ROVING REFERENCE ASSISTANCE

Many public and academic libraries are realizing that just answering questions at the reference desk is not enough. They encourage the staff to move about the reference room to assist users with OPACs and CD-ROMs, with search strategies, and with finding material on their topic. This is often called the "augmented reference service" or "roving reference."

Eileen H. Kramer, a reference librarian at the Frank E. Gannett Memorial Library at Utica College (NY), was working in a two-tiered system with students answering basic questions and referring users to librarians who were "on call" behind an enclosure. Kramer decided to do a study on roving reference to determine its effectiveness. She roamed the reference area during the time periods when she was on call. She found, first of all, that there was almost no overlap between the roving-reference encounters and the traditional reference encounters, and that she could reach more users by roving than she could under the traditional reference desk deployment,[5] in which the questions tended to be directional. As a roving reference librarian, Kramer helped users choose databases (she often found them using the wrong database), and she taught them to refine their search strategies since many did not take advantage of database thesauri or more complex search strategies such as the limit option, truncation, or Boolean searching. She also assisted users in selecting new subject headings in order to get the best search results.

Kramer found that roving-reference encounters are more than twice as likely to result in working with electronic resources. She further reported that by roving she was more likely to help students with the OPAC and CD-ROM databases, and that students with more specific questions such as where to find books on the shelves or specific journal issues went to the reference desk. In her conclusion, Kramer stated:

> "A comparison of the data from my incident log with those from the Utica College Library Reference Desk Survey also indicates that a large proportion of student customers slips away without consulting reference. As these customers vanish, we lose the opportunity to help them construct and launch effective research strategies, and we also lose the chance to help them make the most of powerful but complex electronic and paper resources. . . . Spontaneous customer contact or roving multiplies our opportunities to use our skills and talent and helps us reach the customers we are paid to serve, not just those who approach the desk or make appointments."[6]

Roving-reference work makes great sense in this new library environment. Databases may appear user friendly, but library patrons may not realize that they have not chosen either the best database or the best subject headings. In addition, there is the practical fact that, with workstations so scarce in relation to the demand in most libraries, patrons can be reluctant to leave a workstation and look for assistance. Thus the need for staff to move around the reference room appears to be not an option but a necessity.

There are issues that have to be resolved if roving becomes part of a library's reference service. The library has to decide if roving is part of the librarian's reference desk hours or if it is in addition to the reference desk hours. In addition, the librarian or other staff member must be taught some basic techniques to be effective, such as how to identify users having a problem, and how to offer help in a way that does not make the user feel stupid. It is also a good idea to have identification badges for the staff so that the user knows immediately that the person offering assistance is a staff member.

MAKING REFERENCE MORE USER-FRIENDLY

A reference service is much more than just answering reference questions. The librarian must be able to focus on the user and the user's information needs, which often cannot be clearly articulated in a single reference question. This leads to an emphasis on other activities that until now have often been at the periphery of reference service. These areas include bibliographic instruction or user education (see chapter 3) as well as studying and surveying the behavior of users. Users need assistance with searching electronic databases that often seem user friendly but in reality are quite complex, as well as with using the technology itself—both the hardware and software. Users need guidance in choosing the appropriate resources for a given research project, since studies have shown that many users simply choose the wrong databases to search. Yet the challenges of reaching these users are many. Recent focus groups at Johns Hopkins found that "many people are uncomfortable asking questions; . . . most feel they know how to find information pretty well and can manage the library well enough. . . . [I]n spite of their confidence with their library skills, most have difficulty with basic information retrieval principles and are not aware of many services and resources. . . . [T]aking a class to learn how to use the library, and how to retrieve the information and resources they need, is not a priority with students or faculty. . . . [T]he information desk [is] viewed as unhelpful . . . and the signage is poor."[7]

Librarians must find ways to reach these users who require assistance but are reluctant to ask. This means both creating new models and combining parts of older models. Technology makes it seem as though users can do their own reference work, yet the databases seem simpler to use than they really are. In addition, the user who does not consult a librarian may miss valuable resources. The new models of service will make it easier for users to begin research on their own, will have multiple service points, and will have librarians available for consultation—a "personal shopper" approach. But finding the right mix for each library will be challenging. The sophistication of the users and the complexity of the library will determine what works best.

TELEPHONE REFERENCE SERVICE

Telephone reference has been with us for many years and continues to be an important alternative way for users to request and receive reference assistance. In fact, it may provide an introduction to the library for many. Telephone reference gives libraries the opportunity to speak and have a dialog with users, and to invite users who need more than a short answer to follow up either in person or to request that additional information be sent to them.

Telephone reference is usually confined to factual information that can be read to the patron over the telephone. Some libraries suggest that telephone reference calls be ones the librarian can answer in three minutes, giving both the information requested and its source. If the answer is too lengthy to be read to the patron, the library may be able to fax the response.

Staff must be trained in order to excel at telephone reference. They must learn how to perform a reference interview to determine the nature and specifics of the question. Since there is no face-to-face interaction, active listening is important to be sure that the staff member has not missed some important part of the question.

Telephone reference services are organized in two ways. The first is a separate service in a separate location that is devoted only to telephone reference. In this case, if a question demands a more extensive answer, the user is referred to another desk in the library that can handle it. The second way is for a central desk to answer telephone questions as well as the questions of users that come to the library. The first way is, of course, preferable, but the decision as to how to organize telephone reference will depend on staff available and the number of telephone reference requests. However, a busy telephone reference service should be staffed separately, if at all possible.

Libraries need a policy for telephone reference to assure consistent, quality reference service. The policy should include:

- how telephone reference will be handled during busy periods
- how to respond to requests for verification of multiple citations and holdings
- how long to spend answering each question

- how to deal with questions that are too lengthy for telephone reference
- how to respond to requests for assistance with homework, contest questions, medical/legal questions, and criss-cross directory questions

There are two forms a telephone reference service should develop. The first is a record of questions that helps maintain some consistency in the way telephone reference is handled. The form should include the name and phone number of the caller, the question in brief, the source used for the response, and the resolution of the question (answered/referred). The second form should keep track of statistics, such as the types of questions (such as holdings, citation verification, basic informational, reference), the subject, the level of complexity, and whether the question was answered or referred.

FORM FOR RECORDING QUESTIONS

Date	Name & Phone No	Question	Source Used	Resolution

FORM FOR RECORDING STATISTICAL INFORMATION

Date	Type of Question	Subject	Complexity (ready reference/informational, research; referral, etc.	Resolution

Many urban public libraries have built up their telephone reference services on which users depend to avoid a trip to the library for just a quick question. Among the urban public libraries that have long and well-established telephone reference services are the Enoch Pratt Library (Baltimore, MD), the Brooklyn (NY) Public Library, and the New York Public Library. And now large suburban public libraries have followed suit. For example, the Orange County (FL) Library System staff uses a combination of print resources, their own information files, CD-ROM sources, and Internet sources to answer questions. The library reports that they can answer 70–75 percent of the questions during the user's phone call, referring others to the appropriate subject department. A few are researched by telephone reference and the user is called back. The library offers users the option of delivering the information or answer by mail, telephone, or fax. There is a charge for materials photocopied to be mailed or faxed.[8]

Technology is helping telephone reference departments to do their work even better. They are putting their frequently asked questions in a searchable database to facilitate their work and even putting the database on the Web for library patrons to access. Telephone reference staff also use computers to keep records of questions answered and pending. Many telephone reference departments are also doing an e-mail reference. Even with electronic reference service, however, telephone reference will remain a basic library service. Libraries will continue to offer this service to many of its users who prefer to talk to a librarian than to use the Internet.

ELECTRONIC REFERENCE SERVICE

Reference service is starting to include reaching out to the user rather than the user coming to the library. This may mean e-mail, computerized instructional programs, on-screen guides to assist the user in searching, and listservs.

E-mail is a fairly new medium of communication. It is quick and informal and is characterized by short and even cryptic messages where much is assumed. These characteristics do not necessarily jibe well with reference service, which is based on good communication and complete discussions of the information needed. Nonetheless, e-mail has become an important means of communication, and librarians must learn to deal with the many requests for information that they will receive by e-mail. A 1996 article, "The E-mail Reference Interview," describes five different approaches to the e-mail interview:[9]

1. The *piecemeal approach* is an approach that has no plan. As the user asks a question, the librarian responds. The questions and responses can take place over a long period of time. This spontaneous approach lacks planning and focus, which sometimes results in the librarian losing track of the original question or getting sidetracked into only partially responding to the request.
2. In the *feedback approach*, the librarian asks questions of the user but does not receive a quick response. The librarian goes ahead and does some research in order to get some informa-

tion to and receive feedback from the user. This is not always a successful approach, since it can blur the boundaries of the search.

3. In the *bombardment approach*, the librarian fires off a long list of questions in one paragraph in response to the query from the user. This can be frustrating for both the librarian and the user. The user may be overwhelmed by the number of questions and the format and may not respond to all of them. This kind of approach points out the need for a format for the librarian to use in asking questions that will make it easier for the user to respond.

4. In the *assumption approach*, used to speed up the interview process, the librarian decides that the reference interview is not needed and proceeds on the assumptions which are made based on the user's request. Sometimes the librarian e-mails the user and states the assumptions that have been made. This can be successful if the librarian makes the correct assumptions but depends on the user clearly stating the question.

5. The *systematic approach* is the most organized approach to e-mail reference interviews. When the question is received, the librarian sends to the user either a list of numbered questions to respond to by number or a form to fill out.

POLICY CONSIDERATIONS

Libraries should establish an electronic reference service policy to determine the parameters to this kind of service. For example, the library must decide how much time a staff member should spend on a question and what the user should be told once it is determined that the search is too extensive. A number of alternatives could be suggested, such as advising the user to come to the library to continue the search or referring the user to another library. If the library finds that it gets the same question many times, it can develop some stock answers (FAQs—frequently asked questions) for these situations. The library must also decide how long it will take on an average to produce the information requested so the user will know what to expect in terms of turnaround time (for example, 24 hours). The library also must decide how the service will be staffed: assign each staff member to spend a certain amount of time answering e-mail questions, or assign certain staff to this part of the reference service. Since e-mail questions can come from anywhere, the library must decide whether it will answer all questions received, just the questions received from registered borrowers, or all questions but giving priority to its registered borrowers. In summary, some of the policy issues to be decided are:

- what types of questions will be answered
- whether some stock answers (FAQs) to repetitive questions will be developed
- whether library will respond with an electronic resource or will fax or mail responses to the user
- how long to spend on each question
- which users will be served (registered borrowers only or all who contact the service)

Libraries also can develop some fact sheets and pathfinders to e-mail to the user, depending on the kinds of questions being received. Some basic information on a topic and some guidance as to the reference sources available may help the e-mail user to focus the search and better define the inquiry. Or the library may add links to the library's Web site on subjects of interest to users.

FORM DESIGN AND USE

Designing a form to send to the user can make it easier for the librarian to understand a query and to ascertain sufficient information to respond to the user. The information requested in the form can include:

- personal data—name and e-mail address; other possibilities include address, phone number, fax number, status at the institution/occupation (faculty member, attorney)
- subject—described in a sentence or two or in keyword form, the purpose of the request (for example, a term paper, a company research project), the material the user has found to date, and any other requirements such as languages, the dates of the material, geographical parameters, and formats of material.

FORM FOR RECORDING E-MAIL REQUESTS

Name	
Address	
Request	
Purpose of Request	
Sources Checked	
Special Requirements	
Date Needed	

Many libraries have a designated person(s) who answers the e-mail questions, but larger libraries may use telephone reference to respond to e-mail questions and refer more specific questions to the appropriate subject department.

E-MAIL REFERENCE SERVICE MODELS

The San Francisco Public Library describes its e-mail reference service (INFO) parameters on its homepage (*http://sfpl.lib.ca.us/www/info.html*) (see Figure 2–1). The library states that "appropriate questions are those that can be answered with short, factual responses. We cannot answer questions that require extensive time or research. For this type of question, please call or come in person to use the library's resources. . . . INFO cannot provide comprehensive or lengthy bibliographies, nor can it retrieve or hold library materials for requestors." The page describes how to submit an e-mail question.

Figure 2–1   San Francisco Public Library E-Mail Reference Service

---

INFO, the library's email reference service, will answer specific ready reference questions. *Appropriate questions are those that can be answered with short, factual responses.*

We cannot answer questions that require extensive time or research. For this type of question, please call or come in person to use the library's resources.

INFO staff will only reply via email to the address from which the message is sent to us. We cannot reply to other email addresses, postal addresses, or by phone.

INFO cannot provide comprehensive or lengthy bibliographies; nor can it retrieve or hold library materials for requestors.

In addition, Interlibrary Loan services are not available through INFO. If you would like to borrow or obtain photocopies of library materials, please contact your local interlibrary loan service.

INFO does not answer questions about library polices and procedures. If the information you need is not under "SFPL News and Information" link on the main page, you may call the general information number (415) 557-4400, or contact Community Relations at (415) 557-4277.

Include the following when writing out your question or we may be unable to respond:

- Describe the question or problem to be searched. Be as complete and specific as possible.

- Include in your description the limits or context of the question—e.g., do you need historical or current information; what field of knowledge is the question related to—the who, what, why, when, and where of the question.

- Your name and e-mail address.

<u>Send a Request to INFO@sfpl.lib.ca.us</u>

<u>Return to the San Francisco Public Library Homepage</u>

Reprinted with permission of the San Francisco Public Library.

In the United Kingdom, EARL (Electronic Access to Resources in Libraries)—the Consortium for Public Library Networking (*www.earl.org.uk*)—has developed Ask a Librarian, a national reference service for the public in the United Kingdom. Forty libraries take turns answering the questions posed on this service. Launched in November 1997, the service now receives an average of twenty questions a day—mostly from the United Kingdom, but also from other countries including Singapore, the United States, and Australia.

The Redwood City Public Library (CA) has expanded their electronic reference services to include online forms for a number of library services on their homepage (see Figure 2–2). Users can ask a reference question and receive an answer by e-mail, phone, fax, or mail. Users can also order photocopies of articles via an express service and request both articles and books on interlibrary loan. Fees are attached to the photocopy request ($15) and to the interlibrary loan requests ($2).

Figure 2–2   Redwood City Public Library: Forms Online

Library Home • Contact Us • Search • Help • Site Index • Explore the Internet • City of Redwood City

Reference Desk & Information Services
Ask a Reference Librarian
Card Catalog Online
Citizenship Information
Forms Online
Frequently Asked Reference Questions
Government Information
Index to Periodicals
Information Services Staff
InfoTrac SearchBank
Interlibrary Loan Services
Local History
Outreach Services

FORMS ONLINE
contact: Reference Desk, 650-780-7026
rclinfo@pls.lib.ca.us

The staff at the Redwood City Public Library will be glad to assist you with your information needs. You can use the following forms to contact us over the Internet.

Ask a Reference Librarian	Send us your questions and we will fax, e-mail, phone, or send you a reply.
Comments and Suggestions	Let us know how we are doing.
Document Express Request – Article	Get a photocopy of an article you need—FAST!
Interlibrary Loan Request – Article	Get a journal article from a library outside our system.
Interlibrary Loan Request – Book	Get a book from a library outside our system.
Purchase Request	Suggest a book, video, CD, book on tape, magazine, or newspaper for our collection.

Top of Page

Library Home I Contact Us I Search I Help I Site Index I Explore the Internet I City of Redwood City

Reprinted with permission of the Redwood City Public Library, Redwood City, CA.

The University of Illinois at Urbana-Champaign has a Question Board on their Web site (*www.library.uiuc.edu/ugl/qb*). Answers, including the source, are posted under the heading Browse New Answers; if the source is on the Internet, the URL is given, and if the source is in print, the call number and location are given. The Web page also has a Search Archives button.

Sara K. Weissman from the Reference Department of the Morris County (NJ) Library has been reporting regularly on the library's electronic reference service on the Web, which has been ongoing since 1996.[10] She reports that requests come from both local residents and from people in other states. They often use the service because of distance, bad weather, library hours, or lack of transportation. She says that repeat users are rare and that some users do migrate from e-mail to using the library in person. She advises attempting to answer the question the first time while asking for more information, perhaps giving an encouraging response and then asking clarifying questions. Referring e-mail users to Internet resources is the best way to assist them. She reports what many other libraries have reported: that the response to e-mail reference is not overwhelming and libraries simply have to adjust as they go. However, as libraries highlight their e-mail reference service on their Web site, the number of questions does increase.

E-mail will continue to be a growing part of any library's reference service. Since it seems to grow slowly, libraries have the time to adjust and change as the volume increases. Many libraries have found that their e-mail reference gets more use if they add links in various places in their Web site or highlight it on their Web site. As volume grows, libraries establish tighter guidelines and sometimes dedicate staff member(s) to the services

NEW REFERENCE SERVICE CHALLENGES

DISTANCE LEARNING PROGRAMS

Libraries must consider the realities of many students who are participating in distance-learning programs and need access to the libraries' materials and reference services. The ACRL Guidelines for Distance Learning Library Services state that the suggested services should include: library user instruction, reference and referral assistance, document delivery, and professional and support personnel sufficient to provide quality service. Some of the models established for distance-learning students are the following:

- a department that provides services to distance students with a librarian responsible for the service (this might be a part-time or full-time position)
- an integrated service where distance students are served at the reference desk
- a collection located on a branch campus

Many libraries now provide reference service to distance users through the combination of a Web site, telephone, fax, and mail. A good example is the Florida Distance Learning Library Initiative, a cooperative effort of Florida's state university, community college, and public libraries, which began in 1997 and is composed of reference and referral services, library user training, document delivery, expanded borrowing privileges, and electronic resources. The reference and referral services are contracted for through the University of South Florida Library, which has developed an extensive virtual library that includes a subject guide to databases, detailed explanations as to how to use the databases, maps of the libraries, FAQs on the databases, and electronic reference sources. In addition to this information, there is a special section entitled Distance Learners' Learning Services that tells the distance user how to get needed library services through an 800 number and/or an electronic reference services form on which the user can describe the request for information (see Figure 2–3). The library sees this model as a cross between traditional reference service and the kind of service offered through a software help desk. On the University of South Florida's Web site (*www.lib.usf.edu*), the library has a very simple reference form that students not on campus can use to get reference assistance (see Figure 2–4). The student fills in name, address, university, student ID number, course, professor, and the question, and the library responds to most questions in twenty-four hours. There is an 800 number available for those who prefer voice contact. The library will answer questions by telephone, fax, e-mail, and, of course, regular mail. The staffing consists of two full-time librarians and six part-time librarians working from ten to thirty hours a week. Document delivery service is available to distance learners either through a courier service or through electronic document delivery. A model for borrowing materials from public postsecondary and public libraries near the distance learner's residence is being put in place. Electronic resources are provided at state expense so all college and university students and faculty have access to them and the public libraries as well.[11]

Figure 2–3 Distance Learners Library Services

UNIVERSITY OF SOUTH FLORIDA DISTANCE LEARNERS LIBRARY SERVICES

| Circulation/EReserves | Reference Request Form |
USF Distance Technology & Mediated Learning | Dist.Learn. Reference Referral Center

Currently enrolled University of South Florida students, the faculty, and staff involved in USF distance learning courses are eligible for distance learning library services. The University of South Florida Libraries offer you as a distance learner an array of services similar to those available on campus. These services include:

Onsite borrowing at any of the USF campus libraries and State University System (SUS) libraries (Policies vary.); Remote access to USF's online resources and other services available electronically; USF's Interlibrary Loan/Distance Learning Document Delivery Service; Information and reference assistance both online and onsite.

FREQUENTLY ASKED QUESTIONS

Can I obtain a library card without coming to campus?
Email *mburke@lib.usf.edu* with the following information:
- Your name
- Social Security Number (i.e. your student number)
- Mailing address

Your Patron Barcode Number will be emailed to you so you can begin accessing the USF Libraries without delay. Your card will be sent via the mail.

If you have a card from a previous semester, email Ms. Burke (*mburke@lib.usf.edu*) and she will reactivate your Barcode for you.

If you do not have access to email, you can send your request to
Merilyn Burke, Access Services
Tampa Campus Library LIB 122
University of South Florida
Tampa FL 33620-5400

What kinds of library databases are available?

WebLUIS databases include the USF Libraries' online catalog and many indexing services. FirstSearch, EUREKA, and Lexis-Nexis Universe and over 100 databases are currently accessible online. A number of FirstSearch and WebLUIS databases include links to the full-text of journal articles.

Explore the *University of South Florida Virtual Library* for links to these databases. You will need the active Patron Barcode number as mentioned above in order to use these databases from a remote location. Many databases also require some special browser settings for some remote users. See *Proxy Configuration Notes* for more information.

Do I need a USF computer account in order to access these databases?

You can use USF's computer accounts or you can use an independent Internet Service Provider (AOL, Prodigy, SpryNet, etc.). If you are within a local call of one of the USF modem banks, you can use a USF computer account at no charge. Keep in mind that you will be competing with other students for access to these modems.

USF Academic Computing Departments
Tampa Campus I Saint Petersburg Campus I Sarasota Campus I Health Sciences Center

If you are using a non-USF computer account such as AOL, Mindspring, AT&T, you will need to use the Proxy Configuration Notes in order to access some of the Virtual Library's databases.

(Note: there is some additional Help information about Electronic Reserves policies and procedures including information for faculty who'd like to use this service.)

Where else might I access these library databases?

Florida's State University System Libraries: Since many of our databases were purchased through cooperative licensing agreements with other State University System libraries, many of the Libraries' databases are available onsite at any State University System (SUS). (A few USF databases will only be accessible if you are using a computer which allows you to configure the settings on its web browser.) In some cases you may use your USF ID card to access these services.

Community College and Public Libraries Some databases such as those from FirstSearch and Britannica Online may be available at your local Florida public library as well. Access to these databases was funded through a special appropriation from the Florida Legislature to support distance learning. Continuing access at these sites will depend on funding. More information about this funding is available from Distance Learning Library Initiative "Latest Word on Electronic Resources"....

For locations of libraries nearest you, consult The Dictionary of Florida's Public Libraries put together by the Florida Distance Learning Reference Referral Center.

Figure 2–3 *Continued on following page*

Figure 2–3 *Continued*

Can I get a copy of a book sent to me?

If the University of South Florida Libraries own the book you need to borrow, you can have it sent to you. (Exceptions are materials with limited circulation such as reference books or material from Special Circulations, etc.) Fill out a <u>Regional Exchange Request Form</u> and be sure to check off "BIS/DL" to let the librarians know you are a distance learner.

If you need a copy of a book not owned by USF, consider making your Interlibrary Loan request through your nearest public library or nearest USF campus library or nearest SUS library. (See a collection of <u>USF Library Interlibrary Loan Request Forms.</u>) Non-USF books MUST be picked up at the borrowing library and cannot be mailed directly to you at this time.

Keep in mind that you have checkout privileges at other State University System libraries. The <u>Florida Distance Learning Reference & Referral Center</u> maintains a list of Florida libraries and their locations.

What if I need a copy of an article?

Take a look at the <u>USF Virtual Library InterLibrary Loan</u> for information about specific USF Libraries' policies and procedures. Some restrictions may apply.

- If you need an article, use the <u>Regional Exchange Center Request for an Article</u>. Check the box on that form labelled "BIS/DL" to indicate that you are a "distance learner" and the articles will be mailed directly to you.

Using a fee-based service is another option. Many <u>FirstSearch</u> databases provide you with an option to order journal articles online for direct delivery by fax or mail using your credit card. <u>UncoverWeb</u> also provides online ordering using your credit card, but only has fax delivery.

The <u>Florida Distance Learning Reference & Referral Center</u> can offer advice on the quickest way to order material depending on where you live. The Reference and Referral Center offers toll-free assistance at 1-888-772-8033. See their webpage for a fax number and a web assistance request form.

What are my borrowing privileges at the USF Libraries?

See the USF Libraries' <u>Access Services</u> Policy statements.

What if I want to borrow books from other State University System (SUS) Libraries in Florida?

Your USF library card identifies you to other SUS libraries. You may present your card with its activated Barcode number and obtain borrowing privileges. (Circulation policies such as length of borrowing varies.) There is a List of Community College and SUS Libraries with links to SUS libraries' locations and hours.

How do I get Reference Assistance?

There are a number of ways to get Reference Assistance:

Refer to USF Libraries to get a list of Reference Department phone numbers, locations, library hours, etc. For example, you can call the Tampa Campus Library's Reference Department at (813) 974-2729 (press 1 to get a human being) during the Library's normal operating hours. Library Hours

You can send email to refmail@lib.usf.edu

You can fill out USF's "Ask a Librarian" Request Form

The Florida Distance Learning Reference and Referral Center offers toll-free reference assistance at 1-888-772-8033. See their webpage for a fax number and a web Assistance Request Form.

Related USF Libraries policies and services:
- Circulation and EReserves: USF Libraries
  - See also Electronic Reserves for general information, policies, procedures, etc.
- Interlibrary Loan Policies: USF Libraries
- Tampa Campus Library Access Services Policies (includes USF distance learners)
- Tampa Campus Library Service Request Forms (Interlibrary Loan, Electronic Book Renewal, etc.) (includes USF distance learners)

University of South Florida Virtual Library

Send comments to vlibmail@lib.usf.edu
Copyright 1998 USF Virtual Library
Last Modified Tue, 11/24/98 at 12:08PM

Reprinted with permission of the University of South Florida.

Figure 2–4 Sample Electronic Reference Request Form

Ask a Librarian

The USF Libraries provide electronic reference services. You can send questions on how to do a search, what are the best sources for information, or anything else that you need assistance to do. For specialized areas, you might want to contact the individual libraries that are subject/discipline specific.

Your e-mail address (*required*): _____

Please answer the following questions so that we may process your request more efficiently:

- Are you a currently-enrolled USF student, faculty, or staff? _____ Yes _____ No

- Are you within driving distance of one of the USF campuses? _____ Yes _____ No

- If so, which one? _____

What is your question?

Send the Request   Clear the Form

University of South Florida Virtual Library

Send comments to vlibmail@lib.usf.edu
Copyright 1998 USF Virtual Library
Last Modified Tue, 11/24/98 at 12:00PM

Reprinted with permission of South Florida University.

Many libraries are now providing electronic or digital reference service. Academic libraries vary in their policy as to whether they will answer questions from only members of their community or from the public at large. For example, Boston College only serves its college community, but the University of Illinois at Urbana-Champaign and Roger Williams University both accept questions from the general public. Although most report only a few questions per month, the University of Calgary reported fifty questions per month to its main account and other questions directly to individual librarians. Public libraries have varied tactics for answering questions by e-mail. The Morris County (NJ) Library's HomePage asks "Have a question?" When users click on that phrase, a form appears that the user can fill out with name, e-mail, telephone, the question, and two survey questions—"Do you need to know for business, school report, or personal?" and "How did you hear about this?" (see Figure 2–5). Other libraries with electronic reference service include Fairfax County Public Library (VA), the King County Library System (Seattle, WA), and the Alachua County Library District (Gainesville, FL). These libraries report a 95–100 percent success rate in answering questions, and many are able to respond in twenty-four hours. Though not technically a public library, one of the busiest reference sites is that of the National Museum of American Art (Smithsonian Institution), whose reference service is available through the museum's Web site and through America Online. They average between twenty-five and fifty questions per day and answer 50 percent within two weeks.[12]

Figure 2–5 Sample E-Mail Reference Request Form

Morris County Library

How Can We Help?

Librarians are on duty all the hours we are open. If you prefer, come in and speak to our staff, 9AM to 9PM, Monday through Thursday; 9AM to 5PM, Friday and Saturday; noon to 5PM on Sunday, or call (973) 285-6969 for <u>Reference</u> or 285-6970 for <u>Book Information</u>.

Your name

E-mail (in form xxxxx@yyyyy.com)

Telephone

Your question?

Do you need to know for
____ Business   ____ School report   ____ Personal

How did you hear about this?

<u>Send it in!</u>

<u>Back to front doors!</u>

http://www.gti.net/mocolib1/refbox.html
©Morris County Library
7 January 1997

Reprinted with permission of the Morris County Library, Whippany, NJ.

Libraries are also experimenting with cooperative arrangements whereby a number of libraries support one e-mail site and share the responsibility for answering questions. There is also discussion about forming networks across time zones so that reference questions can be answered twenty-four hours a day. Another level of discussion is whether there should be specialized listservs so that people could ask questions on the appropriate listserv and experts in that area could respond. This leads to the idea of the librarian being an intermediary who matches the expert with the user.

Other new models are still being tested. Several libraries are using the CUSeeMe/Netscape Conferencing that allows for real-time interactive service between a library reference desk and a remote site that might be another part of the institution—such as a laboratory or a dormitory—to communicate with the library's user population. The remote site has a video camera and PC that enables the library to talk to the user and conduct a reference interview. This has been implemented primarily in academic settings such as at the University of California at Irvine and at the University of Iowa. Still other libraries are experimenting with MOO technology and with using an 800 number.

TECHNICAL SUPPORT FOR USERS

Libraries have added a number of PCs to their reference rooms. These PCs may access the library's catalog, the Internet, CD-ROMs, or other electronic products that the library has made available through a gateway such as OCLC, CARL, the Internet, or through a local area network. In order to cope with users' needs for assistance, the libraries have added staff, usually students or support staff who work with the users at the PCs to help them with basic protocols and to troubleshoot technical problems. These staff may be paid or may be volunteers trained by the library.

Another part of the technical support offered library users is what is described as "holistic computing environments." This means that the user is able to use a broad spectrum of tools and databases at a single library workstation. For example, the user can start by using library databases but quickly find the need to research other databases accessible through the World Wide Web. Finally the user can write their report using the research gathered by accessing the word processing software the library has provided.

THE FUTURE: CONSTANT CHANGE

As new models develop, librarians must find ways to cope with an ever-expanding demand for assistance with finding information and dealing with the information overload that often results from the addition of electronic information resources. Many more library staff will have varied roles to play in reference service as librarians delegate reference service into segments that can be handled by nonlibrarian staff. This will mean additional staff training and a commitment on the part of the library for continually updating staff training.

NOTES

1. Cox, "Rethinking Reference Models," [online] available: *www.lib.use.usc.edu/Info/Ref/Cox/rethink_ref/.html*
2. Jackie Mardikian and Martin Kesselman, "Beyond the Desk: Enhanced Reference Staffing for the Electronic Library." *Reference Services Review* (spring 1995): 21–28.
3. Cox, "Rethinking."
4. Telephone interview with Audra Caplan, Assistant Director, Harford County (MD) Public Library.
5. Eileen H. Kramer, "Why Roving Reference: A Case Study in a Small Academic Library," *Reference Services Review* (fall 1996): 70–71.
6. Kramer, "Why Roving Reference," 79.
7. Virginia Massey-Burzio, "From the Other Side of the Reference Desk: A Focus Group Study," *Journal of Academic Librarianship* (May 1998): 210–211.
8. Debra E. Tour, "Quest Line Telephone Reference; A Different Approach to Reference Service," *Public Libraries* (July/August 1998): 256–258.
9. Eileen G. Abels, "The E-mail Reference Interview," *RQ* 35 (spring 1996): 345–358.
10. Sara K. Weissman, "E-ref Characteristics," [online] available: *www.gti.net/weissman;charcter.html* (1998).
11. J. Richard Madaus and Lawrence Webster, "Opening the Door to Distance Learning," *Computers in Libraries* (May 1998): 51–54.
12. Digital Reference Services in Libraries: Current Statistics." Available at *www.vrd.org/AskA/libstats.html*.

3 USER AND STAFF EDUCATION NEEDS

The human element has always been an important part of reference service, and interaction between the librarian and the user has been the key to the entire service. The availability of a well-selected collection of materials, access to electronic resources, and good document delivery are simply not enough. The average user has always needed and continues to need assistance, and it is the reference librarian who has provided that assistance through the traditional reference interview and now through fax, e-mail, and the Web.

Libraries have always provided user education, but in this new technological climate, user education has taken on a new emphasis. As the volume of information increases, users increasingly need the expertise of a reference librarian who is familiar with the electronic reference sources available and knowledgeable about sophisticated search techniques. Librarians also have the task of helping users develop critical thinking skills that will enable them to locate, select, evaluate, and use information effectively. With electronic resources accessible from classrooms, home, office, the dorm room, the laboratory—virtually everywhere—librarians must take into account these remote locations and develop user education for these sites as well as for the library.

Instruction can take many forms. There are many self-help models as well as one-to-one instruction and group instruction. Library instruction also must extend to remote access and distance learners. Users need to learn many skills in order to be able to be able to use both print and electronic resources effectively. These skills include:

- identification of the appropriate materials or databases
- search techniques
- question analysis
- identification of relevant vocabulary
- construction of a search strategy

Users learn best when the learning is related to an immediate information need, when the learning is interactive, when the users participate in the learning process, when concepts as well as techniques are taught, and when current media technology is utilized such as PowerPoint or live demonstrations of electronic resources. By being engaged in active learning, the user begins to think in new ways about information and the process of locating relevant information, and learns how to make better decisions.

WAYS OF PROVIDING USER EDUCATION

SELF-HELP GUIDES AND TUTORIALS

As the burden of library instruction grows, libraries are developing self-help guides and a variety of materials so that users can begin their library orientation on their own. There might be a self-guided tour of the library in print or electronic format that can include information sheets, bibliographies, pathfinders to provide guidance in researching a particular subject area, or a tutorial that the user can read and work through on his/her own. Tutorials can be on the library's Web site or can take the form of e-mail, chat rooms, listservs, or simulations. Many libraries have developed computerized information kiosks to help users find the floor or section of the library they need; after selecting from many subject choices, the user is given information on where a particular subject area or collection is located, often accompanied by a floor plan. Good signage and maps are also part of the self-help instruction libraries have developed. There are fewer questions from users if they have adequate and up-to-date signage to follow throughout the building.

As the number of databases increases, librarians must develop not only more extensive user guides to electronic databases but also subject-based guides that mix print and electronic sources in order to give the user a fuller picture of the resources available. Some possible user guides are:

- computer-assisted instruction models
- resource lists by subject, in print or on the Web
- videotapes/audiotapes
- user guides for specialized research tools, in print or on the Web

Academic libraries have led the way in developing Web-based tutorials. A good example of a tutorial on a library's homepage is that of the Carrier Library at James Madison University (*http://library.jmu. edu*) (see Figure 3–1). This tutorial program—"Go for the Gold: a Web-based program for developing information-seeking skills"—has eight modules each with questions to test the user's understanding of the information:

- Orientation to Carrier Library
- An Introduction to the Information World
- Searching an Electronic Database
- Finding Information Resources

Figure 3–1 Sample Homepage Leading to Tutorial

Module 1—**Orientation to Carrier Library**

Module 2—**An Introduction to the Information World**

Module 3—**Searching an Electronic Database**

Module 4—**Finding Information Resources**

- Using LEO: The Online Catalog
- Background Information
- Books and Non-Print Media
- Periodical Articles
- Biographical Information
- Primary Sources
- Critical Reviews: Book, Movie, Product, Music
- Government Information
- Statistical Information

Module 5—**Using Internet Sources**

Module 6—**Evaluating Sources of Information**

Module 7—**Information Ethics: Citing Sources and Fair Use**

Module 8—**A Search Strategy for Research Papers and Speeches**

About this Program

Send comments to: Lynn Cameron
© James Madison University, Harrisonburg, VA

Reprinted with permission of James Madison University.

- Using Internet Sources
- Evaluating Sources of Information
- Information Ethics: Citing Sources and Fair Use
- A Search Strategy for Research Papers and Speeches

This tutorial provides a wealth of information and clear directions about search strategies as well as suggestions of many different sources to use when writing a paper or a speech. The module on search strategy for research papers leads the user to examine a variety of sources including books, periodicals, newspapers, statistical sources, and government sources. It is well thought out and user friendly.

The University of California, Berkeley, has developed a tutorial on finding information on the Internet (*www.lib.berkeley.edu/Teaching Lib/Guides/Internet/FindInfo.html*). This tutorial provides information similar to that taught in the Internet workshops at the library. It includes an introduction to the Internet, the World Wide Web, and Netscape, a section on how to choose search engines with specific recommendations; information on how to construct and refine searches in different search engines such as Infoseek, Yahoo! and Excite; and a section on other sources of information beyond general Web searching such as subject guides, full-text resources, and discussion groups. This provides assistance for both the beginner and the more advanced user. The very specific information on search engines and how to do searches is particularly well done.

California Polytechnic State University at San Luis Obispo has used a variety of techniques to make their Web-based tutorials more appealing. Students take quizzes based on the information presented. For example, a Web site on smoking includes a quiz to teach students how critically to evaluate a Web site. Tutorials also present various reports on AIDS and ask students to evaluate if they would be appropriate as sources for a paper.

Self-help instruction has its limits, however, since it assumes that the user will spend the time reading and absorbing the information, and it does not fit the needs or answer the more specific questions of many users. It may also discourage the user from going beyond this information to find additional resources.

INDIVIDUAL INSTRUCTION

One-to-one instruction has taken on a more intensive focus with the advent of CD-ROMs, online services, and the Internet. Users must be able to manipulate the equipment and to search the reference tools successfully. Certainly the first level of assistance is to develop and post written instruction at each workstation. These instructions might be on a printed sheet or actually on the computer screen. For some users this will be enough, but others will need a librarian or other library staff member to show them how to get started and how to search a particular database, especially since each electronic resource has different protocols. Sometimes libraries divide this instruction into two parts, hiring nonlibrarian staff to work with users and show them how to use the computer, introduce them to the basics such as using a mouse, and help them understand the way the library's online catalog and Web site works. If the user needs instruction in the use of the databases, the librarian takes over to instruct in choosing the appropriate database(s) for the search as well as the appropriate subject headings and the search protocols of that database. Librarians who do end up working one-to-one with many users should practice what they will say when instructing users in a particular database. Since others may be waiting, it is important to plan how to convey information clearly yet succinctly. In a reference area with computer workstations, librarians and other staff should roam the floor and help users at the workstations since many users don't realize that they need assistance and/or are reluctant to get up and go to a reference desk to ask for help.

Providing individual assistance in electronic resources is often more time consuming than traditional reference assistance—both because the number of reference resources has increased and because it takes longer to explain all the research possibilities to the user. Many librarians say that they spend more time helping the individual user since it is hard to give up on the question when so many possibilities exist.

GROUP INSTRUCTION

Depending on the type of library group, instruction can be tailored to fit the users' needs. Academic libraries have the longest track record in user education. They have long offered courses—both credit and noncredit—in the use of libraries that have encompassed both tours and orientation sessions, multisession courses emphasizing how to use basic library resources, and subject-specific bibliographic instruction targeted at graduate students and faculty.

School libraries also have considered library instruction an important part of their mission. They use both formal and informal instruction to teach students how to use libraries so that they will become more self-sufficient. Some of the basics that are taught include how to use an OPAC, how the Dewey Decimal System works, and how to do searching.

Public libraries have more recently begun to offer more user education, starting with library tours or one-session overviews of the library. With the introduction of CD-ROMs and the Internet, however, the public library has also realized the need to provide user education.

Many public libraries are now setting up labs where users can sit down in front of computers to learn how to use the online catalog, the electronic information databases, and the Internet. Some lacking space train small groups around one computer; others project the information on a screen in a meeting room so that many can participate in the class and supplement the class with a number of handouts.

The Hyde Park Branch of the Boston Public Library introduces small groups of adults to the Internet. The class includes:

- an introduction to the Internet—terminology and history
- an introduction to Web browser software
- how to use the basic computer commands
- how to navigate the Web including surfing, typing in a specific address (URL), searching, using subject guides indexes and directories
- searching techniques
- how to evaluate Web sites
- a demonstration and discussion of how to do searching
- a discussion of subject guides (usually created by librarians) that can be used for more effective searching

A large portion of the class is devoted to search techniques. Often the instructor demonstrates two different searches on two different search tools so that the class can see how different the results can be.[1] Public libraries find that once they have started giving classes, there are requests for intermediate classes and subject-oriented classes such as finding job resources or health resources.

Developing a Training Agenda for Group Instructions

There are many issues to be thought through before training can begin. First of all, there are the goals of the training program. These should be specific enough to be achievable and should be geared to the intended user group. It is easy to include too much material in one training session. For this reason, set out specific goals for each session and adhere carefully to those goals. Too much information will only confuse the users.

The second consideration is the level and content of the training. Not everything can be taught in one or two sessions, so decide what should be included in each session. It is important to gear the curriculum to fit the level of the users. Training can be divided into at least three levels: basic/introductory, advanced, and subject-specific or database-specific:

1. The basic level is for users who have little or no experience with computer searching and is tailored to the needs of the

users. For example, a group of senior citizens in a public library will have different needs from those of a group of college freshmen in an academic library. The basic level for the senior citizens could cover familiarizing them with the computer, teaching them how to use a mouse, how to use the library's online catalog, basic searching skills, how to do e-mail, and how to search the Web for topics of interest such as genealogy, sites for seniors, and the names, addresses, and phone numbers of friends. A basic course for the college freshmen would examine the research process, the advantages of different types of resources, electronic information resources, the evaluation of research material and basic search strategies.

2. The advanced level is for users who have been doing searching but need to refine their skills. This level includes more information about search strategies, such as broadening and narrowing searches, customizing print formats, and proximity operators.

3. The subject or database training level is for those who are working in a particular subject area and need to be able to search one or more pertinent databases. Users should be taught how to select the most appropriate resources to research a particular subject, including journals, nonjournal publications, bibliographic information, and full-text and statistical information. Thesauri and controlled vocabulary used in the subject area should be reviewed as well as the differences in the databases, for example, the depth and scope of their indexing. Information about unique features of databases in the field should also be emphasized.

The third consideration is the teaching methods to be utilized. These methods include single lectures; a formal multisession course; audiovisual presentations using PowerPoint demonstrations, videotapes, audiotapes, slides, and the like; and computer-assisted instruction. Consider increasing the class's involvement in a lecture by incorporating active-learning exercises such as answering a series of questions and brainstorming; such interactive sessions provide the best learning opportunities. User discussion is important and should be incorporated into the teaching method when at all possible so that users learn search strategies rather than just how to search a particular electronic resource.

Single lectures are usually designed to provide an overview but also might be on resources in some particular subject area. Only a limited amount of information can be conveyed in one lecture. A sample single session might include:

- an introduction
- a demonstration by the instructor
- handouts
- time to search with an instructor on site to assist
- a review
- an evaluation

In a formal multisession course, a great deal more material can be covered than in a single lecture. This course must be carefully planned, however, with specific goals for each session. Even within one session there must be a variety of teaching methods—some lecture, some discussion, and the use of video, slides, or PowerPoint. Not everyone learns in the same way, so vary the presentation to allow for different styles of learning and to make the class more interesting.

The training space should, if possible, have one workstation that can be projected onto a screen or, if not, a PowerPoint demonstration that has been prepared in advance. Users should have workstations to use for practice, though it may not be possible to have one for each participant. Try to plan one workstation for each two or three participants (ten to twelve workstations is a good number). Hands-on practice is key to successful learning.

Handouts are an important part of reinforcing any training. They might have an outline of the session, a list of terms and definitions, a list of commands and features, lists of databases to be covered in the session, and sample searches. This provides a way for the users to review the material after they have left the lecture or class.

Evaluate your training sessions to determine if you are meeting the needs of your targeted users. The best way to do this is to hand out an evaluation form at the end of the training for the participants to fill out. Ask users to rate on a scale of 1 (Strongly disagree) to 5 (Strongly agree) statements such as:

1. The session helped me to feel more confident about using the library.
2. The session taught me how to select databases better.
3. The session taught me some basic search strategies.
4. The session was what I had expected.
5. There was enough time to ask questions I had.
6. The handouts reinforced what I had learned.
7. The instructor was well prepared.

At least one open-ended question such as "What would you like to see added or deleted from this session?" or "What was most useful and least useful?" will give the instructor ideas on how to improve the program.

DISTANCE LEARNING

Since many users—particularly those in academic institutions, but also in public libraries and special libraries—do not visit the library often and depend on the resources available through a Web site, the library must find a way to instruct these users. Many libraries are trying new ways to reach their users such as through a listserv where questions can be posed and answered, or various forms of computer-assisted instruction so that users can follow a program to learn new skills. Computer-assisted instruction can use many of the new developing techniques such as the use of color, simulations with sound and animation, group problem solving, automated tests and essays, and tailored learning.

Distance learners comprise an enormous new market that libraries must reach. Among the many strategies libraries have implemented are: using synchronous (real-time) instruction; providing asynchronous (not in real time) electronic instructional materials reinforced by print materials; integrating library instruction into the course curriculum; one-to-one instruction using a toll-free number; and using computer-mediated conferencing systems such as Lotus Notes and First Class to form a discussion group to make students aware of library services. Distance users need lots of assistance—both in getting their hardware and software to work and in finding needed materials. This is a challenging new workload for the librarian.

MODELS FOR TEACHING SPECIFIC SKILLS

At Widener University in Chester, Pennsylvania, librarians Marsha Tate and Jan Alexander have developed a training program on evaluating World Wide Web resources targeted to assist undergraduate students. Training has three components:

1. The students are taught how to evaluate both print and Web resources. Librarians discuss what it means to evaluate accuracy, authority, objectivity, currency, and coverage in a Web atmosphere and discuss other Web-only issues such as distinguishing information from marketing and advertising, evaluating the quality of hyperlinks, software requirements for using a site, and the instability of Web sites.
2. The students evaluate each Web page using a checklist of five basic criteria: authority, accuracy, objectivity, currency, and coverage. The librarians also have developed specific checklists for evaluating advocacy pages, business/marketing pages, informational pages, news pages, and personal pages.
   - The advocacy pages are defined as a Web page sponsored by an organization such as the Democratic Party (*www.*

democrats.org) that have ".org" at the end of their URL.

- Informational pages present factual information such as from colleges and universities and governmental agencies.
- Business/marketing pages are usually sponsored by commercial enterprises and have ".com" at the end of their URL, for example the Coca-Cola Company (*www.cocacola.com*).
- News pages provide current information and also have a URL that ends in ".com." Examples of news pages are USA Today (*www.usa.today.com*) and CNN (*www.cnn.com*).
- Personal pages are published by an individual. The students are shown examples of each type of page and how to apply the checklist to it.

3. The students practice what they have learned using Web pages and the checklists (see Figures 3–2 and 3–3 for the checklists for advocacy and business/marketing Web pages).[2]

Figure 3–2   Checklist for an Advocacy Web Page

How to Recognize an Advocacy Web Page

An **Advocacy Web Page** is one sponsored by an organization attempting to influence public opinion (that is, one trying to sell ideas). The URL address of the page frequently ends in **.org** (organization). **Examples:** *National Abortion and Reproductive Rights Action League, the National Right to Life Committee, the Democratic Party, the Republican Party*

Questions to Ask About the Web Page

Note: The greater number of questions listed below answered *"yes,"* the more likely it is you can determine whether the source is of high information quality.

Criterion #1: AUTHORITY
1. **Is it clear what organization is responsible for the contents of the page?**
2. Is there a link to a page describing the goals of the organization?
3. **Is there a way of verifying the legitimacy of this organization? That is, is there a phone number or postal address to contact for more information? (Simply an email address is not enough.)**
4. Is there a statement that the content of the page has the official approval of the organization?
5. Is it clear whether this is a page from the national or local chapter of the organization?
6. Is there a statement giving the organization's name as copyright holder?

Criterion #2: ACCURACY
1. Are the sources for any factual information clearly listed so they can be verified in another source? (If not, the page may still be useful to you as an example of the ideas of the organization, but it is not useful as a source of factual information.)
2. Is the information free of grammatical, spelling, and other typographical errors? (These kinds of errors not only indicate a lack of quality control, but can actually produce inaccuracies in information.)

Criterion #3: OBJECTIVITY
1. Are the organization's biases clearly stated?
2. If there is any advertising on the page, is it clearly differentiated from the informational content?

Figure 3–2 *Continued on following page*

Figure 3–2 *Continued*

Criterion #4: CURRENCY
1. Are there dates on the page to indicate:
   a. When the page was written?
   b. When the page was first placed on the Web?
   c. When the page was last revised?
2. Are there any other indications that the material is kept current?

Criterion #5: COVERAGE
1. Is there an indication that the page has been completed, and is not still under construction?
2. Is it clear what topics the page intends to address?
3. Does the page succeed in addressing these topics, or has something significant been left out?
4. Is the point of view of the organization presented in a clear manner with its arguments well supported?

Note: This checklist is the original Web version. The author's book <u>Web Wisdom: How to Evaluate and Create Information Quality on the Web</u> contains a revised and expanded version.

Copyright Jan Alexander & Marsha Ann Tate 1996–1999
Copyright Information: This checklist may be freely copied and distributed provided that 1) It is used for educational purposes only, and 2) Credit is given to Jan Alexander & Marsha Ann Tate, Wolfgram Memorial Library, Widener University, One University Place, Chester, PA 19013.

Compiled by: J. Alexander & M. Tate: July 1996
Date Mounted on Server: 5 August 1996
Last Revised: 13 April 1999

If you have any comments or suggestions please contact:
Jan Alexander (<u>Janet.E.Alexander@widener.edu</u>) or
Marsha Ann Tate (<u>Marsha.A.Tate@widener.edu</u>)
URL for this page: http://www.science.widener.edu/~withers/advoc.htm

Return to <u>Evaluating Web Resources Home Page</u>
Return to <u>Library Main Menu</u>
Return to <u>Widener Main Menu</u>

Reprinted with permission from the Website "Evaluating Web Resources," which complements the book *Web Wisdom: How to Evaluate and Create Information Quality on the Web*, Janet E. Alexander and Marsha Ann Tate, Widener University, Chester, PA.

Figure 3–3 Checklist for a Business/Marketing Web Page

How to Recognize a Business/Marketing Web Page

A **Business/Marketing Web Page** is one sponsored by a commercial enterprise (usually it is a page trying to promote or sell products). The URL address of the page frequently ends in **.com** (commercial). **Examples:** <u>Adobe Systems, Inc.</u>, <u>the Coca Cola Company</u>, and numerous other large and small companies using the Web for business purposes.

Questions to Ask About the Web Page

Note: The greater number of questions listed below answered **"yes"**, the more likely it is you can determine whether the source is of high information quality.

Criterion #1: AUTHORITY
1. **Is it clear what company is responsible for the contents of the page?**
2. Is there a link to a page describing the nature of the company, who owns the company, and the types of products the company sells?
3. **Is there a way of verifying the legitimacy of this company? That is, is there a phone number or postal address to contact for more information? (Simply an email address is not enough.)**
4. Is there a way of determining the stability of the company?
5. Is there a statement that the content of the page has the official approval of the company?
6. Is there a statement giving the company's name as copyright holder?

Criterion #2: ACCURACY
1. Has the company provided a link to outside sources such as product reviews or reports filed with the SEC (the Securities and Exchange Commission) which can be used to verify company claims?
2. Are the sources for any factual information clearly listed so they can be verified in another source?
3. Is the information free of grammatical, spelling, and other typographical errors? (These kinds of errors not only indicate a lack of quality control, but can actually produce inaccuracies in information.)

Criterion #3: OBJECTIVITY
1. For any given piece of information, is it clear what the company's motivation is for providing it?
2. If there is any advertising on the page, is it clearly differentiated from the informational content?

Figure 3–3 Continued on following page

Figure 3–3 *Continued*

Criterion #4: CURRENCY
1. Are there dates on the page to indicate:
    a. When the page was written?
    b. When the page was first placed on the Web?
    c. When the page was last revised?
2. Are there any other indications that the material is kept current?
3. For financial information, is there an indication it was filed with the SEC and is the filing date listed?
4. For material from the company's annual report, is the date of the report listed?

Criterion #5: COVERAGE
1. Is there an indication that the page has been completed, and is not still under construction?
2. If describing a product, does the page include an adequately detailed description of the product?
3. Are all of the company's products described with an adequate level of detail?
4. Is the same level of information provided for all sections or divisions of the company?

Note: This checklist is the original Web version. The author's book Web Wisdom: How to Evaluate and Create Information Quality on the Web contains a revised and expanded version.

Copyright Jan Alexander & Marsha Ann Tate 1996–1999
Copyright Information: This checklist may be freely copied and distributed provided that 1) It is used for educational purposes only, and 2) Credit is given to Jan Alexander & Marsha Ann Tate, Wolfgram Memorial Library, Widener University, One University Place, Chester, PA 19013.

Compiled by: J. Alexander & M. Tate: July 1996
Date Mounted on Server: 5 August 1996
Last Revised: 13 April 1999

If you have any comments or suggestions please contact:
Jan Alexander (Janet.E.Alexander@widener.edu) or
Marsha Ann Tate (Marsha.A.Tate@widener.edu)
URL for this page: http://www.science.widener.edu/~withers/advoc.htm

Return to Evaluating Web Resources Home Page
Return to Library Main Menu
Return to Widener Main Menu

Reprinted with permission from the Website "Evaluating Web Resources," which complements the book *Web Wisdom: How to Evaluate and Create Information Quality on the Web*, Janet E. Alexander and Marsha Ann Tate, Widener University, Chester, PA.

The Ann Arbor District Library has created a number of tutorials on its Web site (*www.aadl.org*). Two examples of these tutorials are the "Beginner's Guide to the World Wide Web" and "Searching the World Wide Web." The first concentrates on the basics—defining terminology and a history of the Internet. The second concentrates on the different types of search tools—search engines, subject directories and metasearch engines, general search techniques, and information on each major search tool—Alta Vista, HotBot, Infoseek, ProFusion, Yahoo!, and iSleuth. Other tutorials are on resources for setting up a personal homepage, using e-mail, and browsing Netscape. This library has gone to tremendous effort to provide a great deal of information to its user population (Figure 3–4).

Another interesting example of library instruction is Project TWIST (Teaching With Innovative Style and Technology) at the University of Iowa Library. This three-year, grant-funded project is a cooperative enterprise between librarians and faculty to integrate networked information resources into the classroom. A vital component in this project is an instructional design person on staff who knows the technology process, has a background in pedagogical issues, and acts as a liaison between the library and the faculty. Library staff work one-to-one with faculty to develop a Web page for a particular class. Typically, the faculty member puts the class syllabus on the Web page, has a resource page (often the librarian suggests electronic resources appropriate for the class), may add sound or visual files (such as slides, scanned images), and adds a chat area and a bulletin board. One faculty member put an audio example of a Franklin D. Roosevelt fireside chat on the page along with examples of letters written by citizens to Roosevelt about the speech. The instructors and classes involved have used Web pages as part of the teaching and learning experience with great success. The library's technology also has been used for a face-to-face meeting of students from the University of Iowa and students in Finland using online synchronous chat and the CU-SeeMe technology.[3] For further information, look at Iowa's Web site (*http://twist.lib.uiowa.edu/*).

THE FUTURE OF USER EDUCATION

Future developments in bibliographic instruction will incorporate the electronic, because users want information quickly while they sit at a terminal. One of the best examples of responding better to users' needs is the Gateway to Information at the Ohio State University Library's Web site (*www.lib.ohio-state.edu/*). In this "one-stop shopping," the user learns more about the resources of the library, learns to use the library's resources, and can find the information needed. Users click on the "Gateway to Information" on the Web site and select a sub-

Figure 3–4 Beginner's Guide to the World Wide Web

Using Netscape Navigator

1. <u>Course Objective</u>

2. <u>A Brief History of the Internet</u>

3. <u>The Netscape Screen</u>

   Review of the basic features and functions of Netscape using the ***Ann Arbor District Library*** home page as an example.

4. <u>The Toolbar</u>

   Located across the top of the Netscape screen, this bar contains tools to help you move around the World Wide Web.

5. <u>Hyperlinks</u>

   A connection or link from a page you are browsing to more information on the Internet. This link is often signified by underlined and colored text, as well as a "hand" icon.

6. <u>The URL (Uniform Resource Locator) or Address</u>

   Entering a URL to connect directly to a site.

7. <u>Search Engine</u>

   A way to search for information on the Internet.

8. <u>Bookmarks</u>

   Use bookmarks to save or mark the addresses or URLs of the sites you find interesting.

9. <u>Glossary of Commonly Used Terms</u>

Reprinted with permission of the Ann Arbor (MI) District Library.

ject. The user is then provided with a large array of resources—print, online, and Web—on the subject that have been chosen by the library staff. The reader choosing books, for example, is directed to the online catalog; choosing journals and newspapers is directed to online journal and newspaper indexes; a reader selecting other resources is directed to a list of library databases and Web resources on the particular subject. Many think that this is the future of bibliographic instruction—presenting information on the library's Web site that the user can use easily without consulting a librarian.

This movement to bibliographic instruction via the Web site will develop differently depending on the library and its clientele. Academic libraries will be in the vanguard since their clientele is already eager to use electronic resources and to do research without constantly consulting a librarian. Public libraries, with their more diverse audience, will probably move more slowly into this area and offer a more varied menu of instruction tailored to the varied users they serve. School libraries are likely to combine verbal presentations with tutorials on the Web in the foreseeable future, although the TWIST model has potential for school libraries as well.

PLANNING FOR STAFF EDUCATION

Library staff constitute another clientele that needs instruction as new electronic reference tools are introduced in the library.

Staff must have a chance to learn about a reference resource before it is available to the library's users, who will expect the staff to assist them with it. There are two general models to follow:

1. Assign one staff member to spend some time learning about the new resource and its features. The staff member then makes a presentation to the other library staff that allows time for them to discuss this new resource—its strengths and weaknesses. The staff then agrees on a date for introducing it to the library's users, keeping in mind the time frame necessary for the staff to become familiar with the new resource.
2. A large library can hold a series of workshops to introduce staff to a new product so they can get familiar with the content and the searching techniques.
3. Some companies producing electronic products will come to the library and do a demonstration for the staff. After the demonstration the staff will need time to use what they have learned before they begin working with the public.

An interesting point to keep in mind is that a recent study showed that, although most academic library staff receive CD-ROM and Internet training, many do not receive basic PC training. This gap in their knowledge often hinders their efforts to use the Internet effectively.[4]

The Jackson Library at the University of North Carolina at Greensboro has a full-time staff member in charge of staff training who has developed sessions on a wide range of topics—from file management and the basic operation of a computer, to using MS Office and other specific software products, to HTML and Web page design. Staff members can sign up for as many or as few sessions as they want. The training sessions include hands-on experience as well as a lecture and demonstration. Individual sessions are also available to staff needing additional assistance.[5]

Because there is so much to learn, many libraries are now developing lists of competencies that their staff need in order to work effectively on a reference desk. In addition to understanding the policies and procedures of the library, the staff must know how to search the OPAC, CD-ROM products, and the Internet. Since staff on the reference desk are not necessarily librarians, guides need to be developed to assist this staff in helping patrons effectively. At the Sterling C. Evans Library at Texas A&M University, the staff developed a guide that outlined subject areas for the majority of questions asked. For example, under Mythology/Folklore the subdivisions are:

1. Identification of deities
2. Symbolism
3. Customs, holidays, festivals
4. Summaries of myths and legends.

The Zoology Subdivisions are:

1. Scientific and common names of animals
2. Basic information on animals
3. Illustrations and photographs of animal life
4. Endangered species and field guides."[6]

These guides are developed according to what is known as a knowledge-based approach. They contain the information to answer frequently asked questions, but not in a question-and-answer format. The staff also identified "a list of 'most frequently used print and electronic sources' . . . with sample questions that can be answered by using these sources . . . [and] . . . a list of 'most frequently asked questions' with titles of sources, regardless of format, that will contain the answers."[7]

Staff training needs in using electronic resources will continue to grow at all levels of staff. Libraries must be committed to continual staff training if they are to provide good service to their users. The techniques already discussed for training groups of users apply to staff as well. Staff need to learn in a group setting where there is a chance for hands-on training and group discussion. They too must learn concepts as well as techniques. All staff must be trained in the basics no matter what their position as there will be more opportunities for staff at all levels to work with users. Among the skills staff must learn are:

- to use a word processing program such as Word
- to use a spreadsheet program such as Excel
- to learn some hardware and software basics so that they can troubleshoot basic computer problems
- to use the library's online public access catalog and to learn searching techniques
- to learn the basics about the library's electronic databases

These are only a few of the training programs to be found in this new electronic environment. Review tutorials can also be made available to staff on the library's local area network.

Training and instruction hold the key to this new electronic environment. Both staff and users need to learn how to work with catalogs, electronic databases, and the Internet. They may begin with a group session and then continue to learn through online tutorials or one-to-one instruction. This is a new and complex environment that often appears user friendly but in reality is quite complicated. Librarians must share their knowledge and skills with both users and other staff in their institution.

NOTES

1. Stephanie Goodliffe, "Notes of a Successful Internet Trainer," *Internet Trend Watch for Libraries* (November 1997): [Online] Available: *www.itwfl.com.*
2. Marsha Tate and Jan Alexander, "Teaching Critical Evaluation Skills for World Wide Web Resources," *Computers in Libraries* (November/December 1996): 49–55.
3. Telephone conversation with Karen Zimmerman, Project Director, TWIST.
4. Teresa E. Kirkpatrick, "The Training of Academic Library Staff on Information Technology within the Libraries of the Minne-

sota State Colleges and Universities System," *College & Research Libraries* (January 1998): 51–59.

5. Justin Ervin, "Training Staff at the University of North Carolina, Greensboro," *Internet Trend Watch for Libraries* (November 1997) [Online] Available: *www.itwfl.com/uncg.html.*

6. Candace R. Benefiel, Jeannie P. Miller, and Diana Ramirez, "Baseline Subject Competencies for the Academic Reference Desk," *Reference Services Review* (spring 1997), 88–90.

7. Ibid., 86.

4 PLANNING FOR THE FUTURE

The changes described in previous chapters involve many aspects of reference: the materials, reference service and patterns, user education, and staff education. Even though a great deal is already happening, libraries need to continue to plan for change so that the available dollars can be used to their optimum effectiveness. Decisions will be based on the rate of change that can be handled at the library, the formats of materials the library can handle, the hardware and the infrastructure available, and the changing needs of the users and what that means in terms of changing library service. Planned change is essential—both in terms of the funds available and in terms of training staff to deal with new formats and new service models.

The library will want to develop goals for the improvement of service and the incorporation of technology. These goals might include providing:

- accurate and reliable information
- timely access to the information requested
- access to a wide range of information resources beyond the walls of the library
- access to information resources at the lowest possible cost
- electronic availability of the library's resources so that users can access the library's resources at home and at work in addition to in the library
- user education

Planning for change requires evaluating each aspect of the library's operation and identifying areas for improvement and development. This chapter discusses ways to accomplish this. It looks at how to evaluate:

- the library's collection and develop a collection development policy
- the library's services and find out what the public wants
- user education needs
- the library's staffing and whether staff can be used to better advantage
- what new materials and services to offer in the future

COLLECTION EVALUATION AND DESELECTION

Collection evaluation is an important aspect of collection development; the addition of electronic resources does not change this. Electronic resources must be assessed using the following criteria:

- coverage of subject
- accuracy of content
- currency
- ease of use
- ability of the library to implement the technology

Evaluation is harder with electronic resources than with print because the librarian must sit down at a computer and evaluate the resource. Although the content may have been acceptable when the electronic product was purchased, it may not be now due to changes in the subject or better products available. CD-ROMs in particular are prone to dating, so if a CD-ROM product has not been updated, the library may not want to continue to hold it if its information is not timely. Just as with print material, the library should seek another electronic resource with more current material. Web sites also must be deleted if they are not updated regularly.

An electronic resource must be user friendly or librarians and users alike will choose other sources. And if the technology used for the electronic resource is out-of-date, the library may be forced to abandon it due to the lack of equipment on which to run it—the electronic resource may require technology that is beyond the library's capacity. These are just a few basic reasons why libraries must evaluate their electronic resources and discard some and add others. Figure 4–1 demonstrates a chart format that can aid in this task.

Figure 4–1 Evaluating Electronic Resources

Electronic Resources	Proquest Direct	Health Refernce Center	Business Source
Content			
Accuracy			
Currency			
Ease of Use			
Tech. Requirements			
Price			
Special Features			

Other criteria might include both quantitative and qualitative techniques. The main method of quantitative evaluation is the actual use of the electronic databases, and most vendors now provide these statistics to libraries. There is also software available for counting the number of hits on the library's Web site. These statistics will give the library good information as to the popularity and use of various databases and of the library's Web site. Another quantitative measure is to evaluate the coverage of various subject areas by electronic resources, which can indicate if there are some subject areas over- or under-represented by electronic resources. Lists of recommended electronic resources can be referred to in order to determine what titles other librarians consider to be core titles for an electronic resource collection (this is the electronic equivalent of retrospective collection development tools). Libraries might also want to compare their holdings and growth with libraries of similar size. Qualitative evaluation can be done by using surveys, focus groups, and interviews. These can be structured to give feedback to the library as to how users are using electronic resources, what they want the library to buy or lease, and what problems they experience. See more detail on qualitative evaluation later in this chapter.

COLLECTION DEVELOPMENT POLICY CONSIDERATIONS

New formats require alterations to the library's collection development policy. Although the guidelines for choosing electronic formats may remain similar to those of print (such as for accuracy, currency, objectivity), there are many new aspects to consider. For one thing, this part of the collection development policy may change more often than other parts. Yet it is important to write them down and to revise them as needed. Some of the issues to be examined are:

- guidelines for choosing the format and what formats will be added
- how the reliability of the publisher affects decisions
- the importance of currency
- the relationship of print and electronic products
- the ease of use
- access, including limitations both of the library and vendor
- technical compatibility and equipment required
- cost and predictability of pricing
- use and demand for the resource
- how decisions about redundancy will be made
- role of cooperative collection development, consortial arrangements

The procedure(s) for resolving these and other issues should be documented in the collection development policy. It can be a separate section at the end of the policy, or it can be integrated into the policy.

FORMATS

A primary consideration in a collection development policy is when and how to utilize new formats. Examples of those that should be discussed in a collection development policy are electronic journals, Internet resources, CD-ROMs, online resources, and digitized materials. The library will want to state which formats it plans to add, and why and how it will make decisions about new formats. These decisions might consider what role the demand for resource plays, how hardware affects it, the size of the database, the need for updating it, and so forth.

The library's decisions about format will first of all be based on content. If a reference resource is specialized with a limited audience, the policy might state that it will be purchased as a CD-ROM if available; if the resource is an index with full-text articles that will be used by many, then the policy might state that usually an online or Web product is preferred. The policy might state that if the electronic format is an enhancement to the print product, then the electronic format would be purchased. Enhancements might include better searching capabilities, or interactive features such as sound or video.

RELIABILITY OF THE PUBLISHER

The reliability of the publisher or producer is very important. The collection development should state that the library will try to acquire materials from publisher that it knows have the financial capability to continue to produce the electronic resource and that have the capability to archive retrospective material. The library may also state that it tries to acquire products where there is customer support, such as on-site training and effective manuals.

CURRENCY

If an electronic version is more current than print, it is often the preferred version. But sometimes currency is not a factor if the reference tool covers a subject that does not date quickly. The collection development policy should state when currency is a factor in collection development and perhaps give examples of subject areas where currency is tantamount and areas where it is not as important.

RELATIONSHIP OF PRINT AND ELECTRONIC SOURCES

The question of when to buy print versus electronic products is a crucial one for libraries and needs perhaps the most careful evaluation. There are many issues to document. The library should state if it will always prefer to buy resources in an electronic format if available. If not, then the library needs to define what other factors it will consider, such as cost, demand for the material, or lack of enhancements.

EASE OF USE

The collection development policy will no doubt state that ease of use is one factor in its purchases. The policy may state that the product must be easy for the librarian and the end user to learn. Easy-to-understand screen displays and good help screens are needed, as are a search engine and interface that are user friendly.

ACCESS ISSUES

The access issue concerns the restrictions the library itself has defined, or those resulting from the contract with the company. Restrictions might be limiting the number of concurrent users due to the few workstations or on the inability of the library to provide remote access to the database for the library's users. The policy might state what kinds of vendor-imposed restrictions make a product unfeasible for the library and what are acceptable.

TECHNICAL COMPATIBILITY

Compatibility issues are one of the most complicated considerations in the choice of electronic resources. Library staff must work with technical staff to decide what is feasible within the institution's existing technology infrastructure. For example, CD-ROMs that run well on their own may not perform well on a LAN. When electronic resources are networked, many problems can arise, ranging from problems with search commands to problems with printing. The library may want to state when the technical requirements of a particular piece of software will make it impossible to implement in the immediate future.

Equipment is a crucial part of the use of electronic products. Although it may seem best to convert as many reference materials to electronic resources as possible, it may not be feasible if the library cannot add enough workstations. The policy may state how the library decides to add new electronic products in relation to the number of workstations available.

COST AND PRICING

Cost is another factor to consider. Is the electronic version more or less expensive than the print version? If the cost is greater, are the enhancements worth the additional cost? Or do other reasons justify the additional cost? Perhaps the print version of the reference work is often mutilated or stolen and must be replaced. The library's decision may be to lease and not to purchase; as a matter of fact, leasing is sometimes the only possibility. Some databases are inexpensive as CD-ROMs but prohibitively expensive online. But if cost is comparable or the enhancements substantial, then the library may decide to purchase Web access. Many databases are priced by the number of simultaneous users a library needs and whether the library wants to make the database available to its users from remote locations, and others are based on a per capita figure. Libraries may also consider joining or even establishing a consortium that can negotiate better prices for online or Web-based databases. The library's collection development policy will want to discuss how decisions are made in relation to price and also how decisions about joining consortium are reached.

USE, DEMAND, AND REDUNDANCY

The library might want to state in its collection development that when the material is of limited use, the library may choose paper or CD-ROM, but that when broad use is needed, they may opt for online or Web resources with remote access. The issue of redundancy must also be explained—that the library may decide to buy only the electronic resource unless the library deems it important to have the resource both in paper and in an electronic format.

COOPERATIVE COLLECTION DEVELOPMENT AND CONSORTIAL ARRANGEMENTS

In addition to local collections, libraries will enter into many agreements with other institutions and organizations to share electronic and digitized resources. How these resources fit into the library's collection development should be addressed in the policy. The library should state how selection is made when there are many institutions involved and what parameters the library sets for these agreements. A list of the main points in information the International Coalition of Library Consortia's "Statement of Current and Preferred Practices for the Selection and Purchase of Electronic Information" is on page 123. This statement outlines what the coalition considers fair practices on the part of vendors.

Writing the electronic formats component of the collection development policy encourages librarians to think through carefully what their guidelines should be. This includes reviewing both the current collection and user needs. Once these parameters are established, librarians will find it easier to make consistent selection decisions. This policy should be made public so that the library's users can ascertain the criteria the library uses to make its decisions. Having a policy in place also supports requests to the funding source, be it a governmental unit, a university, or a private organization, for increased funds to support these future directions. Figures 4–2 through 4–5 give examples of electronic resources policies.

**Figure 4–2 Sample Electronic Resources Policy:
The Tampa-Hillsborough County Public Library System**

MATERIALS SELECTION POLICY; ELECTRONIC RESOURCES

Addendum to Collection Development Policy; Approved 3/23/98

GOALS:
The Tampa-Hillsborough County Public Library System provides reference resources in electronic formats to customers in support of our systemwide goals of being:

- The Hillsborough County gateway to worldwide information and resources.
- A customer-driven library which responds to the information and educational needs of the community.

In order to achieve these goals, we aggressively pursue providing appropriate technologies and secure user-friendly databases at all library locations as well as through remote access.

RESPONSIBILITY:
Electronic products are selected within the context of the overall Materials Selection Policy. The Electronic Resources Committee (ERC) provides input to the selection of on-line reference products purchased for systemwide use by suggesting, evaluating and making purchase recommendations to the Collection Services Section.

ERC identifies and selects appropriate reference sites, search engines and tutorials to be linked to the Desktop Reference section of the THPL (Tampa-Hillsborough Online Resources) Home Page. In addition, it provides content recommendations for the THPL Intranet.

Site coordinators at the Main Library and the Science Library at MOSI (Museum of Science and Industry) suggest, evaluate and make purchase recommendations to the Collection Services Section for products to be offered on CD-ROM towers at those agencies. Purchase recommendations for products to be offered on non-networked computers are made by site coordinators at those individual agencies. ERC is informed of products selected but has no active role in the recommendation process.

Automated Services staff provides technical advice on the compatibility of recommended products with the existing infrastructure.

ERC, together with the Collection Services and Automated Services Sections, are responsible for investigating emerging technologies and future delivery methods in a networked environment.

SELECTION CRITERIA FOR ELECTRONIC RESOURCES:
The following evaluation criteria are considered when making purchase recommendations for electronic resources:

Content:
    Age Level
    Authority
    Accuracy
    Comprehensiveness & Depth of Treatment
    Graphics
    Indexing Scheme
    Language
    Multimedia
    Objectivity
    Scope
    Subject Area
    Timeliness

User Interface:
    Clarity
    Graphical and Audio Interface Capability
    On-line Help
    Output Capability (E-mail, Print, Save File, etc.)
    User-friendly Design of Search Engine

Technical Considerations
    Capability for Dial-In and Remote Site Access
    Compatibility with Existing Infrastructure
    Method of Delivery (format or software)
    Patron Authentication Capability
    Response Time
    Time Required for Maintenance

BASIC ELECTRONIC PRODUCTS AVAILABLE SYSTEMWIDE
Broad-based, current electronic products are acquired and made accessible at all library locations and via access to THOR to meet the general, basic information needs of library customers of all ages. These products supplement the resources available through the Suncoast Free-net, THPL Home Page as well as those provided through the Florida Distance Learning Network (FirstSearch and Britannica Online).

Figure 4–2 Continued on following page

Figure 4–2 *Continued*

Recommended types of "core" electronic resources include:

    Dictionary
    Encyclopedia
    General magazine resource
    Basic health and medical information
    Newspapers
    Bibliographic/reviews source for books & periodicals
    Business profile source
    Social issues source
    Literary criticism source
    Science resources
    History and geography
    Biographical source
    Consumer information
    General government/legal information

CD-ROM TOWERS

CD-ROM towers at the Main Library and the Science Library at MOSI provide multiple simultaneous users with access to electronic products that more narrowly focus on specific subjects than those offered systemwide.

Recommended types of products selected for CD-ROM towers include:

Main Library

Products elected include specialized subject indexes, directories, informational databases, etc. which support and enhance the reference activities of one or more of the subject departments. Commercial products as well as those received through the Federal Depository Library Program will be considered for installation on the tower. Major selection emphasis is on products that support reference service to adults. Products, which support basic juvenile reference and reader advisory service, are also considered.

Science Library at MOSI

Science and technology related products appropriate for both the juvenile and adult audience are selected.

NON-NETWORKED COMPUTERS

Highly specialized or research-oriented CD-ROM products with a limited audience are made accessible on non-networked computers at the Main Library and other designated agencies to support unique programs or clientele.

Examples of resources selected include:
    Genealogical databases
    Fund-raising and grantsmanship products
    Products supporting the literacy program
    Specialized Federal Depository Library Program products

Reprinted with permission of the Tampa-Hillsborough County Public Library System, Hillsborough County, FL.

Figure 4–3 Sample Electronic Resources Policy: Morton Grove (IL) Public Library

WORLD WIDE WEB SITES

In response to advances in technology and the changing needs of the community, the Morton Grove (IL) Public Library endeavors to develop collections, resources and services that meet the cultural, informational, recreational, and educational needs of Morton Grove's diverse, multicultural community. It is within this context that the Morton Grove Public Library offers unlimited World Wide Web (WWW) access to the Internet and its multitude of resources. To facilitate the use of the Web in navigating the Internet, The Morton Grove Public Library has established a Web Home Page *www.Webrary.org/NetCloak.acgi$iinside/colldevadultwww.html* that not only highlights the Library and its services, but also presents a subject-approach to selected WWW sites.

WWW sites, provided as links on the Library Home Page, are selected to enrich, broaden, and complement the print and audiovisual library materials. These online resources may be selected to provide home or in-library access to types of material available in print form at the Library or they may be selected to provide more current and more esoteric material than that available at the Library. In selecting resources available on the Internet, the Library attempts to use to its full advantage the unique nature of the Internet by providing government databases for reference needs, sites for hobbyists and pop culture fans, online museum resources for art lovers, and fun activities for both children and adults.

Influencing Factors

The Internet Public Access exists to serve the informational, education and recreative needs of the Library community. Quality and validity of the information, access, design, and its up-to-date nature are deciding factors in the selection of a World Wide Web site on the Internet.

Selection Plan

Standard professional print publications are increasingly publishing reviews of online resources. *Internet World* and other computer-related journals, as well as general interest magazines and newspapers regularly have articles or features on the best Internet resources. These should be considered the first step for assigned Library staff in choosing sites for the WWW. Criteria for the selection of Web sites for the Morton Grove Public Library include the following: 1) Sites should originate from the creating or responsible institution, not a third party. 2) Sites maintained by individuals should be closely monitored. 3) Materials should be up-to-date, preferably with a date and e-mail address available. 4) When dealing with controversial topics, sites with differing points of view should be provided whenever possible. 5) Information should be verified if source is unknown. 6) Sites should be examined and reevaluated regularly for the quality and validity of information, access, design and currency of content.

Retention & Weeding

Each subject area should be fleshed out by the assigned selector with useful, accurate, informative links. Each Web site should be evaluated before incorporation into the Library Home Page for validity and timeliness. Each site should be reviewed weekly according to the assigned schedule in order to maintain working links to Web sites. As links become inactive or out-of-date, they should be removed immediately from the Home Page.

Development Plan

As resources on the Library's Web Home Page are links to many resources that are constantly changing on the Internet, the Library's Home Page too will be constantly changing in design and content in response to the demands of the Internet and its global outlook upon the world.

REFERENCE CD-ROMS

The CD-ROM reference collection exists to supplement the print reference collection. Factors in selection include reference value, space allocation needs, and patron demand. Priority items will be those products which provide added value to their print equivalents, (e.g. indexes which search several years or combine a variety of search factors), products which provide a unique service, and products which combine on one or two discs the equivalent of large paper collections.

Influencing Factors

The CD-ROM collection exists to serve the educational and informational needs of the community, as does the print reference collection. Strong interest in health, business, and consumer information indicate a need for current CD-ROM, tape-loaded, or online products in these areas. The collection should also reflect the academic needs of students at the junior high level through college, particularly in the areas of science and current events. Changing technology will play a role in the choices made; the Internet and other online sources may prove to be the access route of choice for certain information.

Selection Plan

Standard reviewing journals, such as *Library Journal* and *Booklist*, are the tools of choice for professional reviews. Staff will make every opportunity to see demonstrations of potential titles at conferences or at other libraries before purchasing. General interest magazines and computer magazines, which review CD-ROMs, will be consulted to maintain awareness of public demand. Catalogs from publishers and distributors and patron recommendations will be used to identify new titles of possible interest.

Retention & Weeding

An essential consideration in selecting reference CD-ROM products is timeliness. Many of the products currently received are monthly or quarterly subscriptions, which are thus "weeded" automatically. CD-ROM products, which are not automatically updated, will be replaced by newer

Figure 4–3 *Continued on following page*

Figure 4–3 *Continued*

editions as they are issued, in consideration of the annual budget allocation for Reference CD-ROMs, or weeded when the information becomes too dated to be of use. Lost or damaged CD-ROMs will be replaced if appropriate.

Development Plan
As more and more CD-ROM (as well as print) reference sources become available on the Web, the library should be able to gradually eliminate CD-ROMs as a reference source.

Reprinted with permission of the Morton Grove Public Library, Morton Grove, IL.

**Figure 4–4 Sample Electronic Resources Policy:
Blue Ridge Regional Library (Martinsville, VA)**

COMPUTERIZED INFORMATIONAL FORMATS
Computer databases and information in CD-ROM formats are acquired by the library using the same criteria as other materials purchased. Consideration is also given to subject matter, quality and timeliness of the data, use of multimedia presentation, ease of use, compatibility with available technology, and whether the information in this format fills a need or supersedes a print source that has been discontinued.

Figure 4–5 Sample Electronic Resources Policy: Virginia Beach Public Library Collection Management Manual

ELECTRONIC RESOURCES COLLECTION POLICY

Introduction
A significant number of information and education electronic resource titles now exist. Each one has strengths and weaknesses to consider before selecting it for purchase for use in our libraries. The collection development policy serves as the guideline for purchasing print and audio-visual materials and can be expanded to do the same for electronic resources purchased or leased for use in our library system.

If we accept the inherent value of applying present collection development criteria to the evaluation of whether to acquire a particular electronic product, we then need only to add a supplemental set of technology-based criteria to the evaluation process. The additional basic criteria to be applied in scrutinizing electronic products involve issues of 1) content, 2) user interface, 3) network capability and 4) system resources. These criteria will include all site-specific technological requirements and media specific evaluative measures.

Standard product evaluation tools, such as published reviews, user studies, journal articles, and product demonstrations will be consulted as part of the evaluation process. Choosing the best resources for our library depends on knowing our customers' and staff's needs.

The enhanced access that electronic databases provide our customers is well worth the additional time and effort required to review and evaluate electronic resources.

Content Criteria
Customer and programmatic needs are the prime consideration in the selection of an electronic resource. Special attention is given to products that provide coverage of high priority and under-represented subject areas and to subject areas that have a demonstrated need for access unique to the electronic format.

An electronic resource must meet the same overall information criteria as print material. Furthermore, the electronic product should offer more access and functionality than its print counterparts. Electronic products often cost more than the equivalent print source, and each new addition places a strain on the network and other limited system resources. Therefore, an electronic resource must provide added value and be more than simply the print resource in electronic format. The product under consideration must also be compared with the scope and cost of other electronic products currently available.

Figure 4–5 Continued on following page

Figure 4–5 *Continued*

There are a number of additional criteria to consider when selecting an electronic resource. Is this a purchase or are we only leasing the resource? What is the overlap with printed resources already in the collection, do we lose any information we now have if we replace our print tools with this product? What is the time span covered? What is the frequency of updating? Do the earliest years roll-off the database as new years are added? Does the number of discs increase as the database grows? Is it necessary to retain some or all of the print or microforms now in our collection?

User Interface Criteria
We must clearly identify which customer and staff groups will use the electronic resource and what benefits they can expect to derive from its use. In the evaluation process we must consider the ease of use and depth of information levels appropriate for the intended user group. The search capabilities must be suitable for the identified customer group.

Special features and search techniques that are unique to a product must be examined fully to determine if the product fulfills the claims of the producer. The multimedia features should be intelligently built into the total design to expand the usefulness of the product while aiding the customer in its use.

Consideration must be given to how well the customer is guided through the environment by the products. User-friendly features, such as on-screen instructions and guides, as well as on-line tutorials, must be available. Instructional materials and in-house training should be provided by the manufacturer if extensive training is required for staff and customers. It is crucial for Collection Management and Public Service agencies to define and incorporate staff and customer training needs into the final evaluation process.

Networks and Remote Access Criteria
One of the major advantages of an electronic product is that it can be linked via a network of multiple workstations for access by a number of customers at one time. Networking greatly expands the usefulness of a product throughout a building via a Local Area Network (LAN) or throughout the library system via a Wide Area Network (WAN). In order to maintain an equitable distribution of resources in the library system, significant consideration will be given to products that can be used on a network.

Another feature unique to the electronic format is the capability of remote access to the database from home or office computers. The availability of this feature will play a significant role in the decision process.

The selection of an electronic resource involves an element that doesn't exist with print resources. The purchase or lease of an electronic resource includes a definition of the user population allowed to access the product. The access may be limited by the number of concurrent users or limited to a specified number of physical access points. The cost of the product is often determined by the user limits listed in the licensing agreement.

System Resources Criteria
The evaluation of every electronic product includes the determination of what equipment and network capability is needed to operate the new product. The product and its operating requirements must be compatible with the equipment already owned by the library or we must plan to upgrade present equipment and software or purchase new equipment and network software. This necessitates dialogue, planning, and agreement between Collection Management, Automated Services and public service agencies.

Technical support and maintenance from the vendor or producer of a product is a major feature to be weighed in the evaluation process. It is essential to know if they will assist in the installation and setup of the product. Expert trouble-shooting assistance must be available at times that are reasonable and convenient to our staff and customers.

Used with permission of the City of Virginia Beach Department of Public Libraries.

ACCESS DEVELOPMENT POLICIES

Libraries are also developing a new kind of policy called an "access development policy." This has been necessary because all the information needed by the users is not always found in the library. The issue of access can be incorporated into the electronic collection development policy by describing how the library will access information from the Internet for its users, and by perhaps discussing subject-by-subject what resources will be accessed.

For example, Ohio Public Library Information Network (OPLIN), has as its purpose and goal "to acquire electronic resources and develop electronic resources, for the use of Ohio public library customers . . . and to select quality resources to provide to the public libraries and residents of Ohio." OPLIN has developed an Electronic Resources Selection Policy Statement outlining three levels of priority in selecting resources:

1. Level 1 resources are "those which OPLIN will strive to offer to Ohio public libraries at all times." They include:
   - an OPLIN-licensed, full-text, general periodical database
   - an OPLIN-licensed, full-text, general encyclopedia
   - freely available, Internet-accessible, State of Ohio information published by the state or by private organizations
   - freely available, Internet-accessible, State of Ohio public library catalogs
   - OPLIN documents and publications
   - freely available electronic resources that support the diverse educational and informational needs of the residents and businesses of Ohio
2. Level 2 resources are to be "selected to ensure a robust basic selection of resources in each identified Level 2 area." They are:
   - a full-text, multimedia, general encyclopedia
   - a multisource, full-text, K–12 database
   - federal government information
   - OPLIN-licensed or OPLIN-developed databases that provide information about the State of Ohio
   - OPLIN-licensed or OPLIN-developed databases that support the diverse educational and informational needs of the residents and businesses of Ohio
3. Level 3 resources "will be added based on demand, budget and the quality of specific available resources." They are:
   - resources that are otherwise cost prohibitive for most public libraries

- resources through which OPLIN can obtain consortium pricing for member libraries
- resources that appeal to a specialized audience, use experimental technologies, or are available in beta test phase

OPLIN also lists the criteria it examines in evaluating electronic resources:

- purpose. What is the goal of the resource?
- audience. Who is the intended target of this resource?
- content. Is the information factual, and is it original?
- accuracy. Is the information accurate, and does it provide a balanced point of view?
- authority. Is the resource provided by a reputable publisher, organization, or expert, and is the information verifiable?
- currency. Is the resource static or dynamic? If static, is this appropriate to the content? How frequently is the resource updated?
- scope. What are the subject areas and types of material covered? Aspects of scope may include: breadth, depth, and time.
- uniqueness. Is the resource available in other formats? What advantages do this particular resource and format have? What extra features have been added?
- stability. Has the resource been available consistently since its inception?
- format and appearance. Is the format of the resource intuitive and clearly organized? Is there a logical arrangement? Are the most important content features easy to find? Do its visual elements enhance the resource?
- workability. Is the resource convenient and effective to use? Aspects of workability include: user friendliness, searchability, and connectivity (how reliably and quickly the resource can be accessed with standard equipment and software).
- cost. How valuable is the information included on such a resource?

The OPLIN policy also states that there will be a re-evaluation before each contract renewal as well as quarterly reviews. Resources may be replaced at any point if they no longer meet the selection criteria. The policy states that the responsibility for selection rests with OPLIN's Webmasters in conjunction with OPLIN task forces, committees, and the executive director, with final decisions to be made by the OPLIN board.

REFERENCE SERVICE EVALUATION METHODS

Reference services—including ready reference, in-depth reference work, telephone reference, reference service by fax, and e-mail reference service—and the reference collection need to be re-examined frequently as the library's users gain access to more technology and want different and sometimes enhanced services and prefer collections in different formats.

The following general questions can be asked of any service:

1. What do we want to know about?
2. Where do we want to be?
3. How will we know if we are getting there?
4. How close are we?
5. So what?
6. What's next?[1]

In order to evaluate present services and identify new needs and interests, libraries must continually conduct evaluations such as user surveys, focus groups, analyses of reference questions, and user interviews.

SURVEYS

Asking versions of the questions above, surveys can be done in the library, by mail, by e-mail, or by phone throughout the library's community. Whatever the format, it is wise to follow standardized procedures for surveys so that the results are valid and can be used effectively with groups outside the library. Libraries can hire a consultant to help them with the study, or they can do it themselves. If funds are limited, the library should have the consultant train library staff or volunteers in survey and focus group techniques. Most experts on evaluation recommend that more than one method of evaluation be used in order to get a more complete picture.

Surveys have several purposes:

1. They can help identify what collections and services are used and what are needed that are not presently available.
2. By asking questions about the use of the library's collections and services, surveys can publicize the library's collections and services. For example, in querying users as to which of the following collections they refer—books, periodicals, newspapers, videos, CDs, and electronic resources such as CD-ROMS

and resources available through the OPAC—the library can alert the people being surveyed to these resources.

3. Third, surveys can also help the library determine what formats the users prefer and whether they still need the print formats of some materials.

Some examples of the survey questions are:

- What subjects do you use most often or need?
- Are you willing to do research in the library?
- Do you need to borrow material?
- Do you need current or retrospective information?
- Do you use print materials, CD-ROMs, Internet, etc.?
- Do you ask librarians for assistance?

The Washington State University Library sent a twenty-one-item questionnaire to faculty, graduate assistants and selected undergraduate students.[2] The first twenty were closed-ended and one was open-ended. The questionnaire asked about current services, print materials, and electronic resources. Those responding could indicate the level of satisfaction for each service—very satisfied, somewhat satisfied, somewhat dissatisfied, very dissatisfied, or have not used it/have no opinion. They were also asked to rank how important the service or resource was to their work. The library listed the following goals for the survey: "to determine user requirements and expectations; . . . to educate our users about the possible services and resources available to them; . . . to encourage faculty and student interest in library issues, establishing improved communication between providers and patrons; . . . and to document the needs of the library."[3] The authors reported that "this information [from the questionnaires] can be an extremely useful tool in planning library services, budgeting, and allocating limited resources in planning new services. In addition, surveys help justify library needs, services, and priorities to university administrators, state legislators and others involved in budget allocations. Finally, it is essential to demonstrate to library users that we are interested in their expectations and requirements."[4]

The Hershey (PA) Public Library conducted an information needs assessment to determine the types of technology needed to support the information role of the library. The library wanted to find out four things:

1. Was it meeting community information needs?
2. What was the current usage of computers and the Internet at home, at school, and at work in its community?

3. What were the community concerns relating to information needs?
4. Would new technology attract new users?

The results were most interesting and included the following:

- 27 percent of senior citizens aged 55-plus have computers, with 64 percent using commercial online services. But they continue to need training.
- 50 percent of circulation is juvenile, but only 36 percent surveyed have children 4–17. Internet control is considered more important than Internet access.
- Hobby and leisure information needs ranked highest, followed by business and professional information needs, health and fitness.
- Technology interest was highest regarding adaptive equipment for disabled; 46 percent would use the library more if new information technology were available.[5]

FOCUS GROUPS

Libraries are finding that focus groups produce different information from surveys because they allow users to interact with each other. As a result of what others say, users may contribute ideas that would not have occurred to them if they were individually filling out a survey. For example, one user might voice the wish that the library had more spoken word material. Other users might agree, although they might not have thought of this if the first user hadn't spoken up. Focus groups also act as a public relations tool. They make those participating realize that the library is interested in their opinions and others'.

In an effort to better understand the needs of its users, the Carroll County Public Library (MD) conducted focus groups of its users. They asked the groups:

- Why do you use the library?
- How have the reasons or ways you use the library changed over the past few years?
- What services could the library provide to help you take advantage of the recent developments in the electronic delivery of information?
- How could the library serve you better?

The results indicated that the users wanted both the traditional library services and the new technology. Based on input from the focus groups and the staff, the library arrived at a vision statement most of which directly impacts on the delivery of reference services:

> Carroll County Public Library will:
>   Continue to serve the community by offering a broad range of services designed to foster the love of reading;
>   Be the essential contact for all Carroll County residents, agencies, and businesses in need of information;
>   Serve as a gateway to a dynamic global network of information sources;
>   Strive to locate and deliver information and resources efficiently, accurately, and in the format requested by our customers; and
>   Provide excellent customer service by a trained and committed staff.[6]

The Johns Hopkins University Libraries conducted six focus groups to find out what their users wanted and how to meet their needs.[7] The information sought from the focus group participants was:

> Descriptions of experience in retrieving information in the library, including the kinds of problems they had and what they did when they ran into a problem; how they learned to use the library; what they thought of the staff at the service desk—did they ask them questions, did they like to, what did they utilize staff for, and what was the experience like; how they felt about their skill in using the library; what they did not know; and what value did they place on learning how to use the library.[8]

The author, Virginia Massey-Burzio, concluded from the results of the focus groups that "reference departments should . . . focus on putting their resources where they will have the most impact, that is stronger liaison with library users to understand their need and preferences. This includes not only ongoing user studies, but also a focus on eliminating as many barriers to library use as possible, brief, user-friendly instructional assistance at point-of-need, marketing professional staff and resources, and a commitment to evaluate information provision over instruction."[9] She further stated that librarians must give up their ideas and listen to the user and that "we need to focus on our core mission, namely, making it possible for people to get information easily."[10] Massey-Burzio is a great advocate of focus groups not only as a means for getting a level of information not readily available from other sources but also as a way for users to know the library cares about their ideas and opinions.

The New York University Bobst Library held a series of focus groups in order "to gather specific information about the University community's attitudes toward the Bobst Library and to elicit ideas for future library services."[11] Information was gathered on the following topics: teaching, learning, and research in the next ten years; use of the library in course work; personality of the Bobst Library; satisfaction with library services; use of other libraries and information resources; suggestions for the perfect library; suggestions for enhancing the library's value in the NYU community; and library priorities for the future. Focus groups were held with undergraduates, graduate students, faculty, administrators, and library staff. The result of the focus groups was the development of "New Directions for NYU Libraries; Three Year Plan; 1997–2000," which identified seven strategic goals:

- provide collections that meet and anticipate the diverse needs of the NYU community
- simplify, enhance, and expand access to information
- empower users to use information critically
- provide a library facility that meets the academic community's needs
- foster an NYU community that values and uses the NYU libraries and that encourages the development of partnerships with students and faculty
- provide expert library staff to improve the quality of library service offered to the NYU community
- identify and realize new sources of revenue

OTHER METHODS

Other options for evaluation are analyzing statistics collected at the reference desk, keeping track of questions asked at the reference desk by subject, and doing interviews with library users.

PUTTING IT ALL TOGETHER

MATERIALS

Using the information gathered from the surveys and focus groups, the library can begin to put together a plan for the next few years. Begin by comparing the budget for reference materials with the statistics you have gathered of materials purchased by subject area to see how well you have spent your dollars. Then evaluate whether last year's budget was well spent in terms of the user input. Are the subjects most heavily purchased the ones the users need?

Particular issues to be considered are:

1. the budget available for materials
2. the need for duplication—print and electronic
3. subject areas most heavily used
4. subject areas seldom used
5. the telecommunication infrastructure
6. space available for new technology workstations

SERVICES

The next area to consider is services. Review the information from surveys and focus groups to get a sense of your users' priorities and how they use the library. Remember it is important to evaluate what the users want and need—not what the librarians think is best for them.

Areas to consider are:

1. speed of reference services needed
2. the need for off-site reference service
3. staffing needed to perform additional functions such as e-mail reference, document delivery, fax reference, and telephone reference
4. what the users want

PERSONNEL

Rethink the deployment of personnel needed in light of the new materials acquired and the changing models of reference service. Most library budgets have few funds for adding new personnel, especially librarians. Libraries can stretch their dollars further if they mix librarians, paraprofessionals, clerical staff, and technology aides. Most libraries are using paraprofessionals to do basic reference work, leaving librarians available for more complex reference inquiries. Paraprofessionals and clerical staff can also be used for some of the new or repetitive tasks including basic instruction in using PCs, basic search strategies, assistance with technology problems, and scheduling the use of the equipment. This frees the librarian to answer more complex reference questions and to act as a consultant to users in need of assistance. The key to using this mix of personnel well is training, with layers of new training added from time to time to assure good quality service for the users.

BUDGET

The most difficult aspect of the evolving world of electronic technology is the cost. Libraries are truly struggling with the overwhelming costs of both having enough funding for new technology to meet their user demands and then having sufficient funding to continue to upgrade the hardware and software. Many strategies are evolving to deal with these costs and make it somewhat more affordable for the average library.

As a general rule-of-thumb, many librarians plan on upgrading their hardware every three years. Libraries must decide whether to purchase equipment—knowing that upgrading will be necessary—or to lease equipment, which may allow for more flexibility especially for smaller libraries.

There are other peripheral costs to be considered. For example, users love to print pages and pages from the electronic databases. The library must decide if it will charge or not; if so, will the price be the same as for photocopying. In setting prices, the library needs to include the cost associated with putting a coin or card-operated device on each printer and for adding security devices for both the PCs and the printers as well as the additional maintenance required to keep the equipment up and running.

There are some cost options for electronic information. Many libraries are purchasing electronic information through state contracts or consortium arrangements. For the small- to medium-sized library, this is a better route to go and an economical choice. Consortial buying can result in considerable savings and the possibility of buying more substantial databases. Many models have been developed in the last few years and more are emerging. The Committee on Interinstitutional Cooperation (CIC) includes the Big Ten universities and the University of Chicago, which began with a project to acquire electronic resources in the humanities and to share access and costs. In Virginia, VIVA (the Virtual Library of Virginia) received state funding to develop regional electronic resource centers to share full-text information. Other models include the research libraries in Michigan and the community college libraries in Florida.

Libraries that lease databases on their own should try to calculate the least expensive way. It is to the vendor's advantage to sell databases based on the potential number of users, which could mean they base the charge on the university's faculty and student population or on the public library's population. However, the library should make a case for purchasing databases based on use, starting off with a small number of simultaneous users and increasing it as the use of the database increases. Other possible ways to price a database is the pay-as-you-go way, or the flat fee or fixed price.

MARKETING

Libraries must market their services—especially the electronic services, which are less visible on the surface from the traditional library services. Marketing has to be tailored to each library, because the same marketing plan will not work everywhere. The best place to publicize electronic resources and services is on the Web through the library's homepage. But libraries will also want to include information on their resources and services in print media, including special bookmarks, newsletters, and newspapers. Targeting particular user groups also is important—faculty in an academic setting, and community leaders and business people in a community. This constant marketing of library resources and services is the final and crucial piece in putting it all together.

FINAL THOUGHTS

Libraries have moved in a very short time from being traditional libraries, with collections of printed materials, toward digital libraries, where many materials will be available only on the computer screen. Right now the library is a hybrid.

Libraries are also moving from being materials-based institutions to service-based institutions. In the future, they will need to be even more flexible in meeting the needs of their users. Many users will seldom visit the physical library but will have all the same needs as those who do. Libraries will want to do surveys frequently to determine user needs. They will need to anticipate user needs and plan services to meet those needs.

Because users want access to information itself and not just bibliographies, and because not all users will come to the library, libraries will be supplying more full texts online. Since many users will be introduced to and use the library through the Internet, the library's homepage and the arrangement of its resources will have to be easy to use. In addition, the library must arrange its Web site so that users can choose easily the correct databases for their search. Tutorials on the homepage can help users be more effective finding the information they need.

The role of the reference librarian will continue to be redefined. The librarian will continue to answer questions at the reference desk but will also answer questions by telephone, fax, and e-mail. This "librarian without walls" will consult with faculty, students, community leaders, business people, and governmental officials to help them find the information resources they need.

Needless to say, the librarian will be customizing reference services to meet the need of the library's community of users. This may mean designing Web pages to meet requests for information on community or neighborhood, for small businesses, or for a particular college course.

Librarians' roles will be in constant flux in this new electronic environment. They will utilize to a higher degree their skills of organizing and presenting information and of assisting users in coping with the vast amount of information available. They will spend more time evaluating reference materials, planning presentations both in person and on the Web, and consulting one-to-one with users. But most important their workload and its diversity will increase. Their skills will continue to be needed as the world of information increases in complexity.

Figure 4–6 International Coalition of Library Consortia Statement

Recently, the International Coalition of Library Consortia issued a "Statement of Current Perspective and Preferred Practices for the Selection and Purchase of Electronic Information." The document addressed both current problems and future needs, including:

- continuing the principle of fair use
- permanent archiving of e-information
- responsible publishing that will make access to publications available at reasonable prices
- pricing models for e-information that will reduce the per-use cost of information
- creating ways to measure the effectiveness of e-information in order to justify the expenditure of funds

The statement also addressed such issues as:

- the importance of contracts with consortia to allow for lower per-institution rates
- the importance of multiple and flexible economic models that allow institutions to purchase only the electronic and not be forced to purchase a package that bundles the print and electronic
- the need for access to electronic files as soon as possible after the publication of the journal
- the need for institutions to be able to archive material they purchase or lease
- the need for fair use on both sides—that the library's users must have reasonable access to the information and that the library will take reasonable steps to prevent misuse
- the need for management information about the use of the e-information by users

Source: The full statement can be accessed at *www.library.yale.edu/consortia/icolcpr.htm*

NOTES

1. Charles A. Bunge, "Evaluating Reference Services and Reference Personnel: Questions and Answers from the Literature," *Reference Librarian,* no. 43 (1994): 198.
2. Audrey F. Bancroft et al., "A Forward-Looking Library Use Survey: WSU Libraries in the 21st Century," *Journal of Academic Librarianship* (May 1998): 216–223.
3. Bancroft, "Forward-Looking Library Use," 221–222.
4. Bancroft, "Forward-Looking Library Use," 222.
5. Catherine Alloway and Nancy Davis, "The No-Guess Technology Plan." Public Library Association Conference, Kansas City, Missouri, March 13, 1998.
6. Linda Mielke, "Short-range Planning for Turbulent Times," *American Libraries* (October 1995): 906.
7. Virginia Massey-Burzio, "From the Other Side of the Reference Desk: A Focus Group Study," *Journal of Academic Librarianship* (May 1998): 208–215.
8. Massey-Burzio, "From the Other Side," 209.
9. Massey-Burzio, "From the Other Side," 214.
10. Massey-Burzio, "From the Other Side," 215.
11. "Library Service for the 21st Century: Recommendations for Upgrading NYU's Elmer Bobst Library." Internal report prepared by Leslie Burger, Library Development Solutions, November 1997.

BIBLIOGRAPHY

"ACRL Guidelines for Distance Learning Library Services. [Online] Available: *www.ala.org/acrl/guides/dislrng.html*.

Abels, Eileen G. "The E-mail Reference Interview." *RQ* 35 (spring 1996): 345–358.

Bancroft, Audrey F. et al. "A Forward-Looking Library Use Survey: WSU Libraries in the 21st Century." *Journal of Academic Librarianship* 24, no. 3 (May 1998): 216–223.

Benaud, Claire-Lise, and Sever Bordeianu. "Electronic Resources in the Humanities," *Reference Services Review* 23 (summer 1995): 41–50.

Benefiel, Candace R., Jeannie P. Miller, and Diana Ramirez. "Baseline Subject Competencies for the Academic Reference Desk," *Reference Services Review* 25 (spring 1997): 83–93.

Benton Foundation. *Buildings, Books and Bytes: Libraries and Communities in the Digital Age*. Washington, D.C.: Benton Foundation, 1996.

Billings, Harold. "Emerging Patterns of Collection Development." *Journal of Library Administration* 24, nos. 1/2 (1996): 3–17.

Bishop, Ann Peterson. "Scholarly Journals on the Net: A Reader's Assessment." *Library Trends* 43 (spring 1995): 545–570.

Bunge, Charles A. "Evaluating Reference Services and Reference Personnel: Questions and Answers from the Literature." *Reference Librarian*, no. 43 (1994): 195–207.

"CD-ROM Review." *Library Journal* (November 15, 1996): 96.

"CD-ROM Review." *Library Journal* (June 15, 1997): 107.

Coleman, Vicki et al. "Tiered Reference Services: A Survey." *The Reference Librarian*, no. 59 (1997): 25–35.

Cox. "Rethinking Reference Models." [Online] Available: *www.usc.edu/isd/location/doneny/ref/Cox/rethink_ref.html*

Crawford, Walt. "Paper Persists: Why Physical Library Collections Still Matter." *Online* (January 1998) [Online] Available: *www.onlineinc.com*

Davis, Trisha L. "The Evolution of Selection Activities for Electronic Resources." *Library Trends* (winter 1997): 391–403.

"Digital Reference Services in Libraries: Current Statistics." [Online] Available: *www/vrd/org/AskA/libstats.html*

Dowler, Larry. "Our Edifice at the Precipice." *Library Journal* (February 15, 1996): 118–120.

"Electronic Encyclopedia Update." *Booklist* (November 1, 1997): 496–504.

"Encyclopedia Update, 1998." *Booklist* (September 15, 1998): 250.

Ervin, Justin. "Training Staff at the University of North Carolina, Greensboro." *Internet Trend Watch for Libraries* (November 1997). [Online] Available: *www.itwfl.com.uncg.html*

Fine, Sara. "Reference and Resources: The Human Side." *Journal of Academic Librarianship* 21, no. 1 (January 1995): 17–20.

Franck, Carol, and Holly Chambers. "How Full Is the Full in Full-Text?" Poster Session, American Library Association Conference, June 27, 1998.

Goetsch, Lois. "Reference Service Is More Than a Desk," *Journal of Academic Librarianship* 21, no. 1 (January 1995): 15–16.

Goodliffe, Stephanie. "Notes of a Successful Internet Trainer." Internet Trend Watch for Libraries (November 1997). [Online] Available: *www/itwfl.com/goodliffe.html*

Herman, Douglas. "But Does It Work? Evaluating the Brandeis Reference Model." *Reference Services Review* 22, no. 4 (winter 1994): 17–28.

Kirkpatrick, Teresa E. "The Training of Academic Library Staff on Information Technology Within the Libraries of the Minnesota State Colleges and Universities System." *College & Research Libraries* 59 (January 1998): 51–59.

Klein, Joelle. "Duke Study: Users at Library for Net." *Library Journal* (May 1, 1998): 14.

Koutnik, Chuck, "The World Wide Web Is Here: Is the End of Printed Reference Sources Near?" *RQ* 36 (spring 1997): 422–425.

Kramer, Eileen H. "Why Roving Reference: A Case Study in a Small Academic Library." *Reference Services Review* 24 (fall 1996): 67–80.

Lewis, David W. "Traditional Reference Is Dead, Now Let's Move on to Important Questions." *Journal of Academic Librarianship* 21, no. 1 (January 1995): 10–12.

Madaus, J. Richard, and Lawrence Webster. "Opening the Door to Distance Learning." *Computers in Libraries* 18 (May 1998): 51–55.

Mantell, Suzanne. "Looking It Up Is Looking Up." *Publishers Weekly* (September 29, 1997): 51–57.

Mardikian, Jackie, and Martin Kesselman. "Beyond the Desk: Enhanced Reference Staffing for the Electronic Library." *Reference Services Review* 23 (spring 1995): 21–28.

Massey-Burzio, Virginia. "From the Other Side of the Reference Desk: A Focus Group Study." *Journal of Academic Librarianship* 24, no. 3 (May 1998): 208–215.

Mendelsohn, Jennifer. "Perspective on Quality of Reference Service in an Academic Library: A Qualitative Study." *RQ* 36 (summer 1997): 544–557.

Mielke, Linda. "Short-range Planning for Turbulent Times." *American Libraries* (October 1995): 906.

Oder, Norman. "Cataloguing the Net: Can We Do It." *Library Journal* (October 1, 1998): 47–51.

Pang, Alex Soojung-Kim. "The Work of the Encyclopedia in the Age of Electronic Reproduction." [Online] Available: *www.firstmonday. dk/issues/issue3_9/pang/index.html*

Quinn, Brian. "Improving the Quality of Telephone Reference." *Reference Services Review* (winter 1995): 39–50.

Quinn, Mary Ellen. "Encyclopedia Update, 1997." *Booklist* (September 15, 1997): 251.

Rader, Hannelore B. "Educating Students for the Information Age? The Role of the Librarian." *Reference Services Review* (summer 1997): 47–52.

Reference Announcement Issue. *Library Journal* (November 15, 1998): S3.

Shaugnessy, Thomas. "Lessons from Restructuring the Library." *Journal of Academic Librarianship* 22, no. 4 (1996): 251–256.

Stewart, Linda. "User Acceptance of Electronic Journals: Interviews with Chemists at Cornell University." *College and Research Libraries* 57 (July 1996): 339–349.

Sweeney, Richard. "Creating Library Services with Wow! Staying Slightly Ahead of the Curve." *Library Trends* 46 (summer 1997): 129–151.

———. "Leadership Skills in the Reengineered Library: Empowerment and Value Added Trend? Implications for Library Leaders." *Library Administration and Management* 11 (winter 1997): 30–41.

Tate, Marsha, and Jan Alexander. "Teaching Critical Evaluation Skills for World Wide Web Resources." *Computers in Libraries* 16 (November/December 1996): 49–55.

Tenopir, Carol. "Reference Use Statistics." *Library Journal* (May 1, 1998): 32–33.

Tour, Debra E. "Quest Line Telephone Reference: A Different Approach to Reference Service." *Public Libraries* (July/August 1998): 256–258.

TULIP Final Report. "Executive Summary." [Online] Available: *www.elsevier.nl/homepage/about/resproj/trmenu.htm*

Weissman, Sara K. "E-ref Characteristics" (1998). [Online] Available: *www.gti.net/weissman.character.html*

White, Gary W., and Gregory A. Crawford. "Developing an Electronic Information Resources Collection Development Policy." *Collection Building* 16, no. 2 (1997): 53–57.

Zimmerman, Karen. Telephone interview on TWIST project, University of Iowa.

REFERENCE RESOURCES CITED

AAA Map 'n' Go 4.0. CD-ROM and DVD-ROM. DeLorme Mapping. *www.delorme.com*

Academic Press Dictionary of Science and Technology. CD-ROM. Academic Press, 1996.

Alt•HealthWatch. CD-ROM and Online. Softline Information. *www.softlineweb.com/ethnicw*

The American Business Disc. CD-ROM. InfoUSA. Library@infoUSA.com

The American Heritage Dictionary of the English Language. CD-ROM. Houghton Mifflin.

American Medical Association Family Medical Guide. CD-ROM DK. *www.dk.com*

The American Sign Language Dictionary. CD-ROM. Harper-Collins, 1996.

Associations Unlimited. CD-ROM The Gale Group. *www.galegroup.com*

Bartlett's Familiar Quotations. CD-ROM. Time Warner Electronic Publishing.

Biographical and Genealogy Master Index. CD-ROM. The Gale Group. *www.galegroup.com*

Biography Resource Center. Online. The Gale Group. *www.galegroup.com*

CensusCD+Maps. CD-ROM. GeoLytics. *www.geolytics.com*

Collier's Encyclopedia. Sierra On-Line, Inc. *www.sierra.com*

The Columbia Encyclopedia. CD-ROM. Columbia University Press, 1997.

Columbia World of Quotations. CD-ROM. Columbia University Press.

Compton's Interactive Encyclopedia. CD-ROM. Compton's NewsMedia. *www.comptons.com*

Computer Desktop Encyclopedia. CD-ROM. AMACOM, 1996.

Congressional Universe. Online. *www.cispubs.com*

Contemporary Women's Issues. CD-ROM. Responsive Database Services, Inc., 1997.

CQ.Com on Congress. Online. Congressional Quarterly. Oncongress.cq.com

Current Issues Sourcefile. CD-ROM. Congressional Information Service. *www.cispubs.com*

Dictionary of Art.. Online. Grove. *www.grovesart.com*

Elements Explorer: A Multimedia Guide to the Periodic Table. CD-ROM. McGraw-Hill. *www.mcgraw-hill.com.*

Emily Post's Complete Guide to Weddings. CD-ROM. Harper Collins, 1996.

Encarta Encyclopedia Deluxe Edition. See Microsoft..

Encyclopedia Americana. CD-ROM and Online. Grolier Interactive. *www.grolier.com*

Encyclopedia Britannica. CD-ROM and Online. Encyclopedia Britannica, Inc. *www.eb.com*

Encyclopedia Judaica. CD-ROM. Grolier Interactive, 1997. *www.grolier.com*

Ethnic Newswatch. CD-ROM and Online. Softline Information. *www.softlineweb.com/ethnicw*

Facts on File World News. CD-ROM and Online. Facts on File News Service. *www.facts.com*

Famous First Facts. CD-ROM. H.W. Wilson. *www.hwwilson.com*

Fulltext Sources. Online. Annual BiblioData.

Gale Directory of Databases. Annual. Gale Research, Inc.

GenderWatch. CD-ROM and Online. Softline Information. *www.softlineweb.com*

Grolier Multimedia Encyclopedia Deluxe Edition. CD-ROM and Online. Grolier Interactive. *www.grolier.com*

Hammond Atlas of the World. CD-ROM. Hammond, 1998. *www.hammondmap.com*

IDIOM History. Online. Chadwyck-Healey, Inc. *www.chadwyck.com*

Import/Export USA. CD-ROM. Gale. *www.galegroup.com*

Krumenaker, Lawrence. *Net.Journal Directory.* Hermograph Press, 1999.

Landmark Documents in American History 2.0 CD-ROM. Facts on File. *www.factsonfile.com*

Leonardo da Vinci. CD-ROM. Corbis, 1996. *www.corbis.com*

Masterplots Complete. CD-ROM. Salem Press.

Mayo Clinic Family Health. IVI Publishing, Inc.

McGraw-Hill Encyclopedia of Science and Technology. CD-ROM. McGraw-Hill, 1998. *www.books.mcgraw-hill.com*

Medline Advanced. DVD-ROM. Silverplatter. *www.silverplatter.com/usa*

Merriam Webster's Collegiate Dictionary. CD-ROM Merriam-Webster.

Microsoft Encarta Reference Suite 99. (includes Microsoft Encarta Encyclopedia Deluxe 99, Microsoft Encarta Virtual Globe 99 and Microsoft Bookshelf). CD-ROM. Microsoft Corp. *www.microsoft.com*

Microsoft Encarta Virtual Globe. CD-ROM. Virtual Globe Microsoft, 1998. *www.encart.msn.com*

MLA International Bibliography. CD-ROM and online. Silverplatter. *www.silverplatter.com/usa*

The Multimedia and CD-ROM Directory, 1997. CD-ROM. Grove Dictionaries, 1997.

New Millennium World Atlas Deluxe. CD-ROM. Rand McNally, 1998. *www.randmcnally.com*

Oxford English Dictionary on Compact Disc. 2nd ed. Also Online. Oxford University Press.

Random House Webster's Unabridged Dictionary. CD-ROM. Random House.

Reference USA. Online. InfoUSA. Library@infoUSA.com.

RM. Digital Arts & Sciences, 1995. *www.dascorp.com*

Romeo and Juliet. CD-ROM. Columbia University, 1997. *www.columbia.edu/cu/cup*

Routledge Encyclopedia of Philosophy. CD-ROM. Routledge, 1998. *www.routledge-ny.com*

Scribner's American History and Culture. CD-ROM. Simon & Schuster Interactive. *www.macmillansoftware.com*

Software and CD-ROM Reviews on File; Monthly Survey of Computer Software and CD-ROM Reviews . monthly. Facts on File.

Sorrow, Barbara L. and Betty S. Lumpkin. *CD-ROM for Librarians and Educators: A Guide to Over 800 Instructional Resources.* 2nd ed. McFarland, 1996.

Ulrich's on Disc. R.R.Bowker and Ulrich's International Periodicals Directory. Online. OvidTechnologies, Inc. *www.ovid.com*

Webster's New World Dictionary. CD-ROM. 3rd ed. Zane Publishing.

World Book Multimedia Encyclopedia. CD-ROM. IBM Corp. *www.ibm.com*

Writer's Market. CD-ROM. Writer's Digest Books.

INDEX

A

AAA Map 'n' Go, 16
ABI/INFORM, 15, 38
Academic Abstracts FullTEXT Elite, 16
Academic American Encyclopedia, 27
Academic Press Dictionary of Science and Technology, 36
Access development policies, 112–114
ACRL Guidelines for Distance Learning Library Services, 64
Advocacy web page, 85
Alexander, Jan, 83
Alt•HealthWatch, 34
American Business Disc, 39
The American Heritage Dictionary of the English Language, 28
American Library Directory, 24
American Library Directory on Disc, 16
American Mathematical Association, 37
American Medical Association Family Medical Guide, 36
The American Sign Language Dictionary, 14
Andrew Mellon Foundation, 39
Ann Arbor (MI) District Library, 89, 90
The Annual Bibliography of English Language and Literature , 42
Argus Clearinghouse, 44
Ask a Librarian, 62
Association of Research Libraries Directory of Electronic Journals . . . , 45
Associations Unlimited, 29
Atlases, 30–31
Avery Index to Architectural Periodicals, 42

B

Bailey, Charles W., Jr., 45

Bartlett's Familiar Quotations, 29
Bell & Howell Information and Learning (formerly UMI), 15, 24, 34
Best Information on the Net (BIOTIN), 23
Beyond Bookmarks: Schemes for Organizing the Web, 22
Bibliography of American Literature, 42
Biographical and Genealogy Master Index, 31
Biographical Dictionary, 31
Biographical sources, 31–32
Biography, 31
Biography Resource Center, 31
Blue Ridge (VA) Regional Library Electronic Resources Policy, 108
Booklist, 43, 45
Books in Print, 16, 24
Boston Public Library, Hyde Park Branch, 80
Bowker (see R.R. Bowker)
British Library, 25
Business/marketing web page, 87
Business Source, 16, 24, 38

C

California Polytechnic State University, 78
CARL UnCover, 25
Carnegie-Mellon University, 37
Carroll County (MD) Public Library, 116
CD-ROM Librarian, 44
CD-ROM for Librarians and Educators, 44
CD-ROM sources, 14–16
  evaluation criteria, 15
CensusCd + Maps, 32
CenStats, 32
Chadwyck-Healey, Inc., 15, 24, 42
Chemical Abstracts, 36
Choice, 43
Christian Science Monitor, 38

CINAHL (*Cumulative Index to Nursing and Allied Health*), 16
Circuits (*The New York Times*), 44
Code of Federal Regulations, 32
Collection development policies, electronic, 98–101
Collection evaluation, 96–97
Collier's Encyclopedia, 26–27
Columbia Encyclopedia, 28
Columbia World of Quotations, 29
Commercial database sources, 16–17
    evaluation criteria, 17
Compton's Encyclopedia, 16, 27
Computer Desktop Encyclopedia, 14
Computers in Libraries, 44, 45
Congressional Quarterly, Inc., 16, 24
Congressional Record, 32
Congressional Universe, 39
Consortial arrangements, 101, 120
Contemporary Authors, 24
Contemporary Women's Issues, 39
Cooperative collection development, 101
CQ.Com on Congress, 37
CQ Researcher, 16
CQ Weekly, 37
Current Issues Sourcefile, 39
CUSeeMe/Netscape conferencing, 72

D

Daily Monitor, 37
Database, 45
Database & Disc Reviews, 43
Databases, 43
Dawson Information Quest, Inc., 25
Delorme, 16
Dialog Corporation, 16, 24
Dialog, 17, 34, 38
Dialog Classic, 24
Dictionaries, 28–29
Dictionary of American Biography, 42
The Dictionary of American History, 42
Dictionary of Art, 28
Digital National Security Archive, 15

Directories, 29
Dissertation Abstracts, 15
Distance learning programs, 64, 83
Dow-Jones, 17
Duke University, Lilly Library, 22
Duke University, Special Collections Library, 39
Dun and Bradstreet Information Services, 24
DVD-ROM, 16

E

EARL (Electronic Access to Resources in Libraries), 62
EBSCO Publishing, 16, 24, 34, 38
Eighteenth Century Short Title Catalogue, 42
Electronic reference service, 57–64
    form design and use, 59–60
    policies, 58–59
    service models, 60
Electronic resources
    collection development policy, 98
    criteria, 96
    evaluation, 97
Elsevier Science, 37
E-mail reference (see Electronic reference service)
Elements Explorer: A Multimedia Guide to the Periodic Table, 36
Emily Post's Complete Guide to Weddings, 14
Encarta Encyclopedia Deluxe Edition, 14
Encarta Multimedia Encyclopedia, 14, 27
Encyclopaedia Britannica, 16, 26, 27
Encyclopedia Americana, 26, 27
Encyclopedia Judaica, 28
Encyclopedia of Associations, 24, 27
Encyclopedias, 26–28
Ethnic NewsWatch, 34
Evaluating Internet Web sites, 45
Evaluating Quality on the Net, 45

F

Facts on File, 24, 37

Facts on File World News, 37
Famous First Facts, 14
Fax reference, 65, 68
Federal Record, 32
FedStats, 32
First Search, 17
Florida Distance Learning Library Initiative, 65
Focus groups, 116
Fort Worth (TX) Public Library Criteria for Selecting Internet Resources, 19–21
Fulltext Sources, 45
Funk & Wagnall's New Encyclopedia, 27

G

Gale Directory of Databases, 45
Gale Group, 24, 34
GenderWatch, 34
General BusinessFile ASAP, 38
Geosys, 31
Geology and the Environment, 36
Government information sources, 32
Government Reporter, 16
GPO Access, 32
Grolier Multimedia Encyclopedia Online, 27
Grove's Dictionary of Art, 28

H

H.W. Wilson Company, 13, 16, 25, 34
Hammond Atlas of the World, 30
Health Source, 16, 24
Hershey (PA) Public Library, 115
Humanities Index, 16
Humanities reference sources, 40

I

IDIOM History, 43
Import/Export USA, 38
Indexes, 33–35
    evaluation, 33
INFOMINE, 23

Information Access Company (IAC), 34, 38
Information Quest, 25
International Coalition of Library Consortia, 123
International Index to Music Periodicals Full Text, 16
International Index to the Performing Arts Full Text, 16, 42
Internet Librarian, 45
Internet Public Library, 23
Internet sources, 18–25
    evaluation of free sources, 19

J

James Madison University, 76, 77
Johns Hopkins University Libraries, 117
JSTOR, 39

K

Kirkus, 43
Knowledge Source, 25
Kohl, David, 43

L

LaGuardia, Cheryl, 43
Landmark Documents in American History, 41
Leased electronic databases, 23–25
    evaluation criteria, 24
Leonardo da Vinci, 42
LEXIS-NEXIS, 17, 25, 34, 39
Librarians' Index to the Internet, 23
Library Journal, 43, 45
Library of Congress, 39
Library surveys, 114
Literary Market Place on Disc, 16
Literature Online, 15, 24, 42
LJINFOTECH Online Databases, 43
Lubans, John, Jr., 22
Lycos Road Maps, 31
Lycos Top 5%, 44

M

Macbeth, 41
Magellan Internet Guide, 44
Map 'n Go, 30
MapQuest, 30, 31
Marquis, 13
Masterplots Complete, 41
Math & Science Gateway, 36
MathSciNet, 37
Mayo Clinic Family Health, 36
MAS FullTEXT (*MasterFILE FullTEXT*), 16
McKiernan, Gerry, 22
McGraw-Hill Encyclopedia of Science and Technology, 36
Medline, 16, 36
Medline Advanced, 16
Member Data Disk, 16
Merriam Webster's Collegiate Dictionary, 28
Michigan Electronic Library, 28
Microsoft Encarta Multimedia Encyclopedia, 27
Microsoft Encarta Virtual Globe, 30
Million Dollar Directory, 24
MLA Bibliography, 42
Moody's Company DataDirect, 25, 39
Moody's Financial Information Services, 25
Monthly Catalog of U.S. Government Publications, 32
Morris County (NJ) Library, 64
   e-mail reference request form, 72
Morton Grove (IL) Public Library Electronic Resources Policy, 106–108
The Multimedia and CD-ROM Directory on CD-ROM, 44

N

NetFirst, 23
Net.Journal Directory, 45
New Book of Knowledge Online, 27
New Grove's Dictionary of Music and Musicians, 28
New Millennium World Atlas Deluxe, 30
New York Times, 44

New York University Bobst Library, 117
Newspaper Source, 16
Nicholls, Paul, 44
Nine Planets, 17, 36

O

OCLC, 23
Ohio State University, 89
OhioLink, 3
OneLook Dictionaries, 29
Online, 45
Online evaluation criteria, 17
Online resources, 17
Ohio Public Library Information Network (OPLIN),
   Electronic Resources Selection Policy Statement, 112
OVID Technologies, Inc., 16, 37
Oxford English Dictionary, 28
Oxford Text Archive, 40

P

Phonefinder USA, 16
Prestamo, Anne, 23
Print sources, 12–13
   evaluation criteria, 12–13
Project Gutenberg, 40
Project Perseus, 40
Project TWIST, 89
Project Vote Smart, 37
ProQuest Direct, 15, 24, 33, 34
Publisher's Weekly, 43
PubMed, 36

Q

Questal-Orbit, Inc., 37
Quotation books, 29

R

Rand McNally, 13
Random House Dictionary of the English Language, 28

Random House Webster's College Dictionary, 28
Ready Reference Shelf, 24
Reader's Guide to Periodical Literature, 16
Redwood City (CA) Public Library, 22, 62, 63
Reference & User Services Quarterly, 43
Reference collection development tools, 43
Reference USA, 38
Renaissance, 16
Research consultation model, 48
Reference service models, 47–53
   academic library models, 48
   public library models, 50
Researcher, 16
RLIN (Research Libraries Information Network), 42
RM, 42
Romeo and Juliet, 41
Routledge Encyclopedia of Philosophy, 42
Roving reference assistance, 51–53
R.R. Bowker Company, 16, 24

S

San Francisco Public Library, 60, 61
Scholarly Electronic Publishing, 45
School Library Journal, 43
Schrock, Kathy, 45
ScienceDirect, 37
Science reference sources, 35
The Scout Report, 45
Scribner's American History and Culture, 41
SearchBank, 33
Seattle (WA) Public Library, 22
Self-help guides, 76
SilverPlatter, 16, 25
SIRS Mandarin, Inc., 16, 25
Social Science Index, 16
Social science reference sources, 37
Softline Information, Inc., 34
Software and CD-ROM Reviews On File, 43
SPIPIO, 42
Staff Directories on CD-ROM, 16
Staff education, 91–93
Staffing patterns, 51

St. Ambrose University, O'Keefe Library, 23
State Legislator Data Disk, 16
Statistical Abstracts of the United States, 32
Statlib, 37
STN International, 36
Subscription Books Bulletin, 43.45
Surveys, 114

T

Tampa-Hillsborough County (FL) Public Library System—Materials Selection Policy Electronic Resources, 102–105
Tate, Marsha, 83
Telephone reference service, 54–57
   policy, 54–55
Tenopir, Carol, 43
Texas A & M University, Sterling C. Evans Library, 92
Thesauri, 28
Tiered reference service, 48–50
Tillman, Hope, 45
Training evaluation, 82
TULIP (The University Licensing Program), 3
Tutorials, 76–78

U

Ulrich's International Periodicals Directory, 24, 30
Ulrich's on Disc, 16
UMI (see Bell & Howell Information and Learning)
University at Albany (NY) Libraries, 23
University of California-Berkeley Digital Library SunSITE, 23, 41
University of California-Berkeley Library, 22, 78
University of Illinois at Urbana-Champaign, 64
University of Iowa, 89
University of Michigan School of Information, 23
University of North Carolina at Greensboro, Jackson Library, 92

University of South Florida Distance Learners Library Services, 66–70
University of Virginia Institute for Advanced Technology in the Humanites, 40
U.S. Census, 32
U.S. Code, 32
User education, 75–91
  evaluation, 82
  individual, 78–79
  group, 79–80

V

Vicinity Corporation, 31
Virginia Beach (VA) Public Library Electronic Resources Policy, 109–111

W

Washington Post, 38
Washington State University Library, 115
WebCrawler Map Thyself, 30

Web Resources for Libraries, 23
WebSPIRS, 25
Webster's New International Dictionary, 28
Webster's New World Dictionary of the English Language, 28
WebWatch, 45
Widener University, 83–88
Wilson (see H.W. Wilson Company)
The Wordsmyth English Dictionary-Thesaurus, 28
World Book Encyclopedia, 16, 27
World Biographical Index, 32
World News Digest, 24
World Wide Art Resources (WWAR), 42
World Wide Web, evaluation, 83
Writer's Market, 14

Y

Yahoo, 44
Yahoo City Maps, 31

ABOUT THE AUTHOR

Kay Ann Cassell is the Associate Director of Programs and Services for the Branch Libraries of the New York Public Library where she is responsible for branch library collections, the development of new services, and the implementation of grant-funded projects. She also teaches both information sources and collection development courses as an adjunct faculty member at the Pratt Institute School of Information and Library Science.

Ms. Cassell edits the quarterly journal, *Collection Building*. She co-authored *Developing Public Library Collections, Policies and Procedures: A How-To-Do-It Manual for Small- and Medium-Sized Public Libraries* (Neal-Schuman, 1991) and is a frequent contributor to the library literature. Prior to her present position, Ms. Cassell served as a reference librarian, an adult services consultant, a public library director, and an academic library director.